Praise for
My Hair and ... [?]
New Eve... [?]

Yvette wins the hearts of everyone she meets. Her infectious personality draws people in, and her love for God and others keeps them engaged. I trust you'll find her stories funny, moving, deeply authentic—and above all, glorifying to God. The Lord changes lives, and in Yvette's case, in radical, wonderful ways!"

—Jim Daly, President, Focus on the Family

When Yvette walks into a room, the entire place lights up. She is equal parts authenticity and joy, and audiences can't get enough. Through her message, she will sit with you in your pain, give you cause to laugh, all the while praising the Jesus she loves until you're doing the very same.

—Michele Cushatt, inspirational speaker and author

Yvette adds an extra measure of joy and humor to our team, and she does so in her new book as well. I believe women will see themselves in her stories and learn that what seems like a disaster at first—either big or small—can be turned around and used for God's glory. Well done, Yvette!

—Brady Boyd, Senior pastor of New Life Church

I am delighted that Yvette has written this book! For the last decade, I've wished she would share her amazing story—and her amazing heart. Yvette is one of those special people who can make you snort with laughter while she's illustrating the deepest of lessons about grace, resilience, and implicit trust in God. I was absolutely captivated by this book, and I know you will be too.

—Shaunti Feldhahn, social researcher and best-selling
author of *For Women Only*

Yvette and I have been friends for twenty years, and so I realized a long time ago that she's a joy and wisdom bomb just looking for a place to detonate! She's helped me see Jesus bigger, and I can guarantee this book will help you have a clearer picture of Him too. If not, Yvette will give you your money back plus a pony (actually, I'm only teasing about the pony part).

—LISA HARPER, author, Bible teacher, and Women of Faith speaker

Yvette's story is a profound picture of the loving-kindness of our God. At our greatest moment of need He picks us up, dusts us off, and calls us His child, His beloved. He did that in my life, and He continues to do so with breathtaking beauty and tenderness. If you want to be encouraged to pursue Jesus with all that's within you, I commend this book to you.

— SHEILA WALSH, author of *God Loves Broken People*

The moment we started reading this book, we literally couldn't put it down. It's true that sometimes fact is stranger than fiction—thus the life of our sweet friend Yvette! Her joy is infectious; her stories are compelling. Through these pages you'll learn God is in the details of our daily lives—and it's abundantly evident that He has a fantastic sense of humor! We hope you come to understand He loves us just the way He made us and that life with Him is an outrageous adventure!

—PHIL AND HEATHER JOEL, founders of deliberatePeople

MY HAIR & GOD'S MERCIES...
New Every Morning
A Story of a Life Changed by Grace

Yvette Maher
with Amy Tracy

Tyndale House Publishers, Inc.
Carol Stream, Illinois

To Landon and Jaxon—
You are the first two of my little angel babies, and I am
CRAZY in love with you! I hope this book establishes that your
foundation is built on the Truth of Jesus and that His mercies,
like Nana's hair, are new every morning.

Contents

Introduction

I think you should tell people that you carried a mattress on top of your car from place to place, Tootie." That was my mom's suggestion for what to include in this book—and yes, my nickname is Tootie.

In fact, in my late teens and early twenties, I drove around with a mattress ingeniously secured by a garden hose to my old beater car. The car was missing a floorboard on the driver's side, so I covered the gaping hole with a grill grate from the charcoal Weber in our backyard and lay a floor mat over the whole mess. It came in handy when I needed to dump my soda or a cold cup of coffee. Because the car lacked a muffler and started with a boom, my ride was christened The Bomb.

While I can look back and smile at my nomadic lifestyle, hardship and insecurity were at its root. The intense desperation I felt during my young adult years was no laughing matter.

So why the heck do you care to read about someone you don't know—even if she did have a rock star of a car as an adolescent? If I were Julia Roberts, Oprah, or the superstar of the month, some of you *People* magazine fans (only in the doctor's office, right?) would grab this book to learn more about the details of my life.

As it is, I not only lack the fame of these individuals; I'm not even a one-hit wonder. And yet I have stumbled into God's grace over and over throughout my life. No matter how much I've screwed up or found myself in crazy situations, His mercy has been new *every* morning. He is a God who delights in seeing us pick up our sorry selves and try again. Seriously, knowing that the Lord of the universe has had my back, even in the darkest, most uncertain times, beats having any amount of celebrity status, money, or talent.

My Journey

I am a Kentucky farm girl to my very core.

Tobacco, cow's milk, and probably a touch of horse manure course through my veins. I hail from Waynesburg, a small country town where people are born, marry, raise their families, and die without giving a serious thought to relocating; everyone, that is, except me.

**I am a Kentucky farm girl
to my very core.**

My mom and dad met in high school, and they started dating when Dad was on leave from the Air Force. Though my mom, Yvonne, says they rarely communicated on an intimate level in twenty-five years of marriage, she notes his charismatic personality, humor, and sense of fun. In fact, folks in our area would say that my father, Sharon Dale Greer, never met a stranger.

After my parents married, the Air Force moved them to Texas, where Dad was stationed. Mom stayed for three months, but money problems forced her to find work in yet another state. Warning signs of my dad's infidelity surfaced right from the get-go. Soon after they married, Dad wrote Mom a letter asking for a divorce because he had fallen in love someone else. Mom was heartbroken; like many women of her generation, denial and longsuffering would mark her life.

After my dad served his time in the military, my folks, whose marriage survived the storm of an affair, settled on the Waynesburg farm where my sisters and I were born. (Diana, our eldest sister, says my birth marked the advent of our first indoor bathroom. I seriously believe that my two sisters should be indebted to me for that!)

Farm life was fairly simple. We milked approximately seventy Holsteins morning and night, stuck our arms inside cow uteruses and pulled out calves, canned beans and other veggies in big washtubs over wood fires, and grew tobacco, corn, and hay. We worked hard and ran barefoot spring, summer, winter, and fall.

My sisters and I spent our free time climbing apple trees, playing cowboys and Indians, sledding on a massive metal Coca-Cola sign (which we also used as a boat in the creek during the summers), catching lighting bugs, and soaking up every moment of our county fair in the summers. We'd also turn fifty-five-gallon steel drums on their sides, climb atop, and walk, which would roll them around the farm. But one of our most adventurous and "Can you even believe we made it to our teen years alive?" games was called circus. We'd climb on top of the garage roof, jump on our horses, and ride bareback as fast as we could.

Weekends looked much like weekdays, because they were jam-packed with work. In the early days we'd attend Sunday services at a nearby church, where generations of our family had worshipped. Then we'd come home to tuna fish sandwiches mixed with hard-boiled eggs and pickle relish. On Saturday afternoons we'd stand on the fireplace hearth and sing and dance to *American Bandstand*. We pretended to be Bobbie Gentry, Glen Campbell, and Diana Ross and The Supremes. And when the electricity went out, all of us girls would play Rook or poker by candlelight using matchsticks or Mom's pink curlers as currency.

Each of us worshipped our father in our own way. As I like to say, "Diana was his boy, Sherri was his girl, and I was his favorite." This made life especially hard when my folks split up and Dad moved away. Everything seemed to change overnight, and that made for turbulent teen years.

Through a series of twists and turns—that I'll share in this book—I landed in Colorado Springs, and eventually at a Christian ministry called Focus on the Family. Like everything else in life, I seem to have stumbled into it.

I served in a multitude of positions at the ministry for twenty years, including as a senior vice president and later as the host of a weekly show called *Your Family Live!* Throughout my life, I have been in awe of the Lord's favor and the amazing opportunities that have come my way. There I was a poor Kentucky farm girl from a broken family helping to strengthen parents, marriages, and families of all kinds!

If you have ever wondered how God's grace and mercy can tangibly order your own messy circumstances, this book is for you.

I also have a passion for cooking. For better or worse, and in days of riches and lean pickings, food has played a supporting role in most of my memories. I am brought back to different periods of my life by the tang of a yeast biscuit, the saltiness of fresh-cured ham, and the smell of a freshly baked fruit pie.

Because food and the meals accompanying food are central to who I am, I've included a recipe or two at the end of each chapter. It's a chance for you to connect with my story in a different way and perhaps to whip up a dish and make a memory of your own.

So, if you have ever experienced crazy, unexplainable life events, fear, or unmet expectations, I hope you'll read on. And if you have ever wondered how God's grace and mercy can tangibly order your own messy circumstances, this book is for you.

God delivers on all of His promises. He is a Savior who loves to delve into our unfinished business! May you be encouraged to reach for Him and be tutored by His grace—and may you see His goodness through my words.

one

My Ill-fated Trip
to Starbucks

Here is the world. Beautiful and terrible things will happen.
Don't be afraid.

—FREDERICK BUECHNER, *Wishful Thinking*

By January 10, 2008, it had been about twenty-eight years since my dad divorced Mom. I was forty-six years old, living in Colorado, and pulling into a Starbucks parking lot on a Thursday morning when my cell phone rang.

My sister Sherri blurted, "Dad has shot Sandy."

I had seen Dad and his girlfriend, Sandy, just three months earlier. They were both happy and alive. Not a single bullet hole between them. My numb brain couldn't comprehend this news. "What?" I asked.

"Dad shot Sandy," Sherri repeated, "and his picture is all over the TV news. They say he's armed and dangerous. And there's a manhunt, and the schools are all on lockdown. This can't end well, Tootie; I need you to call Mom. You need to come to Kentucky now!"

I navigated safely into a parking spot; my world was slightly blurry, similar to the fog that descends after receiving one of those dreaded middle-of-the-night phone calls. As I got out of my car, Sherri was still talking frantically, and David, a friend I was meeting for coffee, stood in the doorway of Starbucks, looking puzzled.

At this point my knees buckled, and I saw my mild-mannered friend moving swiftly toward me. My mind was paralyzed by shock, everything playing out in slo-mo.

I must have looked pale, because David placed his arm under my own and helped me step up into his SUV. As I gazed out the front window at nothing in particular, I told him the story in fits and starts. He was in shock too.

"I have to call my mom," I said, "and then I have to fly home."

Speaking to my mom brought on a wave of tears—she and Dad had been divorced for years, yet remained friendly. I was thankful that my two sisters, Diana and Sherri, would be keeping vigil with her.

Tears turned to sobbing, which brought about nausea. I turned to David and said, "I think I'm going to throw up." I climbed out of his SUV, and in front of God and the whole world, I vomited in the parking lot.

Then my sweet, precious friend David, who has a slight stutter—exacerbated when he's nervous—tried to find the right words as he patted me lightly on the back. This act made me smile. I knew he was doing his best in the midst of his own shock over my family crisis, but, frankly, being doubled over in a dress and hose in a parking lot was not my finest hour. We were just supposed to be having coffee!

My father's picture with the words "armed and dangerous fugitive" draped across area TVs.

Thank God David took control and called my superstar assistant, Laura, who made all the travel arrangements and drove to my home to pack my clothes, including a black dress for what was sure to be a funeral. My husband, Tommy, gave me a lift to Denver International Airport, more than sixty miles away. I had about two hours to get there and board.

I had learned from Sherri that my dad shot Sandy three times at close range and then fled the scene on foot. A countywide search ensued, which included school lockdowns, helicopters, dogs, state troopers, and my father's picture with the words "armed and dangerous fugitive" draped across area TVs. (Two years earlier he had completed a ten-year sentence in the state penitentiary for killing the lover of his third wife.)

While Tommy was driving à la Starsky and Hutch toward Denver, Sherri called again. "Diana has gone off on her own," she said. "She's gone to hunt down Dad."

My sister Diana is the spitting image of my father, and like him, she often acts first and thinks later. She and Dad are both known for their hot tempers.

"Diana thinks he may be hiding out at Greer Park (our family's land)," breathed Sherri. "And the news says the area is surrounded by state troopers. She and Dad had a huge fight yesterday. She's determined to tell him she loves him; she says she has to ask for his forgiveness."

"Call her back, Sherri, and tell her to let the police handle it!" I almost shouted. "She does *not* want to live with the visual of Dad in a shoot-out with the cops. I'm almost at the airport. I'll call when I change flights in Chicago."

Boarding my flight in Denver, I had no clue whether my father was dead or alive. As soon as we landed and I got a cell signal in Chicago, I called for an update. The outcome was still uncertain, but Sherri provided a few more devastating details: The police had found Dad, but he had shot himself with a shotgun, blowing off half of his face. Both he and Sandy were on their way to the hospital in Lexington.

We all know life can change in a moment. On January 10—the day of the shooting—I never imagined I'd be pacing Concourse A at Chicago O'Hare en route to my hometown, Waynesburg, Kentucky. But there I was, in the midst of a family crisis involving my dad again.

My morning had started like most others, except for one other major wrinkle that I was still reeling from: Lee, one of my twin daughters, had announced three days earlier that she and her boyfriend had an unplanned pregnancy (I'll tell you about it later). As a result, I was a prime candidate for large doses of prescription meds and perhaps weeks of shock therapy. But through the chaos, I did have one solid thing going for me. I had staked my life on a strong faith in God. I was confident that the God who had guided me through a lifetime of mishaps—both molehills and mountains—would help make order out of the dual dramas unfolding in Kentucky and Colorado. He was a faithful God, of this I was sure.

I did have one solid thing going for me. I had staked my life on a strong faith in God.

I boarded my flight to Lexington, Kentucky, and into the unknown. And I took out my journal and began to write out prayers for all of my family. As I struggled to process what was happening, I remembered scriptures in the Bible like this one:

> Bless our God, O peoples!
> Give him a thunderous welcome!
> Didn't he set us on the road to life?
> Didn't he keep us out of the ditch?
> He trained us first,
> passed us like silver through refining fires,
> Brought us into hardscrabble country,
> pushed us to our very limit,
> Road-tested us inside and out,
> took us to hell and back;
> Finally he brought us
> to this well-watered place.
> —Psalm 66:8–12, MSG

I lived and breathed promises such as this one as the plane ascended to 32,000 feet. And I knew that a peaceful, well-watered place was somewhere down the road.

Kentucky Heartbreak

When I arrived at the Blue Grass Airport, my sister Sherri and my best friend, Lona, were anxiously waiting, and we rushed to the hospital. We found the wing that my father was in; law enforcement officers from every agency in the state surrounded it. I half expected to see the mounted police turning the corner on their trusty steeds.

Sadly, we were refused entry to the ICU wing. If we wanted to see Dad, we'd have to get a judge's order. The Health Insurance Portability and Accountability Act of 1996 (aka HIPAA) prevented the hospital staff or the police from giving us any information about Dad's condition. We didn't know whether he was dead or alive. We didn't know, that is, until we overheard he was scheduled for surgery. We left the hospital thinking that surgery was good news. They wouldn't operate on a dead man.

The next morning, after planning our strategy over much-needed coffee, we manned the phones. After making many calls, we were finally able to find a friend of a friend, who's a judge, to provide us a password that would give us special access to information about Dad's condition.

The password was *giraffe*. (Honestly, who would ever suspect zoo animals?) We called the hospital, gave the nurse the secret word, and she told us the bare-bones information about Dad.

He was alive. And Sandy was alive. They had been healthy just a few months earlier when they had visited my Colorado home. Their current critical medical conditions seemed surreal.

Sherri and I decided to make the hour-plus drive back to the hospital. We were tired of judges, secret passwords, and HIPAA laws. We wanted to see him.

This time we got farther—the ICU waiting room—and straight into the bosom of Sandy's family. They were waiting for Sandy's arm surgery to be completed. We wondered what kind of greeting we'd receive from them. After all, what would you do if you ran into the daughters of the man who came close to murdering your mom two days ago?

What would you do if you ran into the daughters of the man who came close to murdering your mom two days ago?

I approached Sandy's daughter. She was twentyish and looked exhausted and disheveled. "I'm just so sorry," I said. "I don't even know the words to say." She graciously received us.

Because Sandy wasn't in police custody, Sherri and I could legally visit with her. When Sandy came out of surgery, I asked her daughter for permission to see her. The daughter agreed, and Sherri and I put on standard green scrubs over our clothes. We also put on fitted latex gloves and masks and then entered her room.

Sandy was still mentally out of it. She looked awful, swollen, and bruised. Her face, neck, and shoulder were still covered with buckshot from the double-barreled shotgun. I prayed over her and held her hand. We shed our green hazmat gowns, and I loaded Sherri down with our coats and purses. She would work as my Sherpa for this mission. Sherri and I then left. I felt stunned and mournful.

Having been inside the ICU wing, Sherri surmised the unit was shaped like a horseshoe. Dad had to be here somewhere. And I was determined to see him!

We slipped quietly through the hallways like two criminals on our way to a heist. As we rounded the corner near the nurse's station, I spotted two state troopers. Bingo, we were getting warm. We continued to push ahead, and I watched one of the officers walk away; the other was guarding the door.

We ducked into an empty office marked Comfort Room, and each of us took a deep breath. Then I poked my head out the door and spied on the guard through a giant, curved mirror on the hallway ceiling.

"There's a huge cop guarding the door," I said to Sherri as a joke. "You bring him into this room and flirt while I slip in and visit with Dad."

Sherri responded with something to the effect of, "Why do I always have to be the one flirting with the big ol' police officer? How about you do that and I'll go find Dad!"

After this brief moment of comic relief, we left the room kind of tickled, nervous, and frightened all at the same time. Would we actually get in to see Dad? Would the guard kick us out? Arrest us?

We decided to take the high road and just ask the officer if we could visit with Dad briefly.

The guard stepped toward us. "Far enough, ladies," he said. "No visits."

I launched into my spiel about our being his daughters and having come all the way from Colorado. I whispered the code word to him: "Giraffe." I asked if we could talk to someone higher up. He agreed to make a call to his supervisor. Meanwhile, we hit the nurse's station and said *giraffe* again, and we were given an update: Dad had lost an eye. They couldn't save his cheek. They inserted a plate in his jaw so he could eat. He was stable— for now. Just as we were digesting this news, the officer approached and granted us permission for a ten-minute supervised visit.

The police officers searched us and then handed us hospital togs. Once again we suited up in scrubs, gloves, and masks. Sherri and I were pit-of-our-stomachs nervous at this point. Sherri seemed to be paralyzed with panic.

Three days, four hours, and fifteen minutes after the shooting, we entered the hospital room of my father, the man who has caused my heart to swell and fall for so many years. The first things that hit me were the machines and the smell. I inhaled iodine. It smelled cold and sterile. Then I spied Dad lying there so still. It was one thing to hear about his massive facial injuries; it was another to see them. The reality of his situation was sinking in and making me physically ill.

His hair was wild, long, and pure gray, like Moses'. Blood stained his gown, and I noticed the fresh stitching on his sunken cheek.

His hair was wild, long, and pure gray, like Moses'. Blood stained his gown, and I noticed the fresh stitching on his sunken cheek.

He woke up as we approached, and I said, "Hey, Dad, it's Tootie." Sherri and I both leaned over and kissed him.

He said, "Whadya'll doing here?"

"Just checking on you, Dad," I said.

He asked about the kids, and I told him he was going to be a grandpa. "Lee's pregnant, and you've got to get well because you're going to have a new grandbaby."

It was unreal to think that my dad shot and nearly killed someone, and we were standing there exchanging brief snippets of family news. A strong brew of anger and grief, love and hate, bubbled up and made me weak in the knees.

How did we come to this place? After his last stint in prison, he promised never to put himself in that position again. He made solid plans for the years ahead. And now he had blown it all away. Now he was physically suffering to boot. It was almost unbearable. I wanted to shout: "You had ten years in prison to reflect and to dry out from alcohol abuse! Ten years away from cigarettes! Ten years from the wrong kind of women and so-called friends! And ten years to find yourself a new life! What the heck happened?

Dad's downward spiral had begun after he divorced my mother. He was controlling and jealous throughout their marriage. I recently asked her what it was like.

"If he told me to turn right, I turned right," she said. "If he got jealous of my friends at work, I'd quit. I once bought a new car by myself because I was tired of breaking down in the middle of nowhere. He didn't say anything about the vehicle on the phone, but he came home from a week on the railroad and took it for a joyride. A couple of months later, he put sugar in the gas tank and destroyed it."

Dad's subsequent wives (and girlfriends) hadn't quite seen life the same way my mom had. The other women had fight in them. In fact, Irma, the woman he left Mom for, moved out of their mutual house and took everything, every last penny, while Dad was away. He came home to find only a mug and coffee pot left. Irma's selfish act devastated him.

Drugs, alcohol, and rough living took our whole family to very bad places. Soon after Irma left, Dad's brother walked into the local elementary school, found his wife, who was the school secretary, and shot her to death. He then took his own life.

Eventually Sherri's and my time with Dad had to end. The officer jolted us out of our brief but intense conversation with him. "Ladies, it's time to go," he said.

I started crying. Sherri started crying. It was the kind of involuntary weeping where the tears fall fast as rain. "I'm heading back to Colorado tomorrow, Dad," I told him. "And you need to rest and be a good patient. This officer let us in to see you, and he is a good man. He'll be watching out for you. We love you a lot."

Dad laughed in his Dad kind of way, the way I remembered as a little girl. I wondered if he grasped the severity of the situation or had blocked out the events of days earlier. I leaned over and kissed him. Then we walked out. But before we left I hugged that big brown teddy bear of a cop and said, "Thank you so much for being part of our miracle. You'll never know the gratitude."

The officer told me I must know someone in high places to have gotten such approval. I told him that I knew the biggest Boss in the universe, Jesus Christ. The guard responded that he, too, reported directly to this King. We all had tears in our eyes.

Sherri and I left the hospital and walked into the cold Kentucky air.

Travails in Trailers

The experience of visiting Dad had stunned us. Sherri and I hit the closest "watering hole." And in addition to a glass of wine, we needed to plan. First, we had to get an attorney for Dad. Second, we needed to visit his makeshift home, which was a camper, the next day.

Dad's camper was situated on the property of a colorful friend named Huli. Sherri, Diana, and I launched out early the next morning for Huli and Little Huli's farm. Upon arrival we were relieved to find there were no police cars in sight. We spotted Huli and Little Huli in the barn tending to their tobacco crop. Huli was sweet, and he stood up for Dad. They had been friends forever. He was very obliging and told us to go through the camper and take what we wanted.

As I approached Dad's home, another big fat wave of emotion hit me. This stuff was part of his life, his history. And he'd never see any of it ever again. Dad would never see the light of day outside a lattice of barbed wire in a prison courtyard.

I walked through the home in a sentimental haze. Here were his plate and fork in the sink. And there was his breakfast nook with a bulletin board littered with pics of my Colorado family—just me, Tommy, and our kids.

I called my sisters over to the photos: "Just in case you needed proof that I was his favorite," I quipped, pointing at the photos. They rolled their eyes.

Diana walked around collecting things and mumbling, "I've been looking for this Crock-Pot" or "Here's my fishing pole." I explored the shower and looked through his cabinets. What kind of toothpaste did he use? What brand of soup did he buy for himself? I wanted to see the little details that made up his routine. I wanted to make those connections with my own habits. In spite of his horrific crime, he was still my dad, my blood.

As we loaded up his belongings in trash bags, including several flannel shirts, my Grandma Thelma's Bible, a vacuum cleaner, canned goods for Mom—basically, our inheritance—I felt sick to my stomach.

A flood of emotions and thoughts has enveloped me since this event in 2008. My dad is daily reminded of his transgressions as he serves a life-plus sentence in federal prison. As his daughter, I have asked myself, "Who the heck is this man?" I mean really, *Who is this man?* It's hard to separate logic from emotion, and yet as a somewhat rational adult, I can see and smell the craziness in all of this.

Even now, I'm angry, hurt, disappointed, and mostly sad. I'm sad for Dad. Sad for me. Sad for my sisters and Mom. And sad for my community of friends and family in my small Kentucky town.

Relationships and Grace

But let's get back to angry. How is it that the deepest emotion of love can run so closely to the emotion of, dare I say, hate? I love my dad, but I hate him for the suffering, pain, and strife he's caused me and countless others. Yes, I'd take a bullet for my father . . . but I also want to choke the life out of him from time to time. I'd like to think I'll find peace or resolution for this conflict on this side of heaven, but it's unlikely. Some parts of life are just messy. And I believe that God is in the midst of messy, gray areas and unfinished business.

Some parts of life are just messy. And I believe that God is in the midst of messy, gray areas and unfinished business.

At the same time, I'm smitten by grace. It's only by the grace of God that I can open the letters my dad sends to me and visit him each and every time I'm in Kentucky. It's only by grace that I can pray for him when sometimes I want only to lobotomize all memory of him. And it's only grace that allows me to authentically grieve for his loss and the brokenness that has consumed him.

Our family members are part of our identity, our story. We can't write them out of our history. Therefore, we have a compelling need to redeem our histories, which prompts us to extend grace to family even through horrific circumstances.

So what does *grace* mean? It's often defined as "unmerited divine favor." Author Philip Yancey writes, "Grace means that there is nothing we can do to make God love us more . . . or to make God love us less."[1] He says, "Grace, like water, flows to the lowest part."[2]

I show kindness toward my dad because he's my dad, not only because I have this love-hate thing going on, but also because I have been the recipient of unmerited favor throughout my lifetime. As my mom likes to say, "more times than you can shake a stick at." Yep, I've blown it over and over on dinosaurian and microscopic levels and every stratum in between. And it's the memory of that favor, the memory of those second and third chances that keeps me extending it to my dad and others. (Keep reading and you'll see many of my own failures.)

Grace means taking positive action even when our hearts aren't touched or moved and our feelings are less than benevolent. Then grace becomes an act of obedience to God.

Sometimes I blow it still, though. My comfort comes in knowing that even when I fall short, God does not. He is there each and every time with forgiveness and that indescribable, unmerited favor for me yet again.

HOT ARTICHOKE AND SPINACH DIP

Sherri and I consumed a large amount of this delicious stuff after leaving Dad in the hospital.

Ingredients
- 1 cup thawed, chopped frozen spinach
- $1^1/_2$ cups thawed, chopped frozen artichoke hearts
- 6 ounces cream cheese
- $^1/_4$ cup sour cream
- $^1/_4$ cup mayonnaise
- $^1/_3$ cup grated Parmesan cheese
- $^1/_2$ teaspoon red pepper flakes
- $^1/_4$ teaspoon salt
- $^1/_4$ teaspoon garlic powder

Directions
1. Boil spinach and artichokes in 1 cup of water until tender.
2. Drain and discard liquid.
3. Heat cream cheese in microwave for 1 minute, or until hot and soft.
4. Stir in rest of ingredients and serve hot.

two

Sitting in the V

When we realize life can't give us what we want, we can bet-
ter give up our foolish demand that it do so and get on with
the noble task of loving as we should. We will no longer need to
demand protection from further disappointment. The deepest
change will occur in the life of a bold realist who clings to God
with a passion only his realistic appraisal of life can generate.

—LARRY CRABB, *Inside Out*

Okay, is there anyone quite like Carol Burnett? Ask anybody: I love her! Who can forget lines like these? "Mama always said: 'No matter what you look like, you can always write.'" And one of my favorites: "Comedy is tragedy plus time." So true! Meeting her tops my bucket list. Seriously, how much would I have to pay for an introduction?

Besides being one of the funniest ladies alive, Carol Burnett has been to hell and back and hasn't lost her sense of humor. In fact, the hardships of growing up with an alcoholic dad, living through a painful divorce, and losing a child and spouse have given her humor a bittersweet depth.

Carol Burnett also holds a special place in my heart because my dad and I shared a love for the *The Carol Burnett Show*. Every night after a long day of farm chores, he'd lie on his side on the couch, and I'd plant myself in the V of his legs. In the span of an hour or so, we'd share the intimacy of laughter. In fact, whenever my dad saw anything funny on television and I could hear him laughing, I'd run into the TV room to share the moment.

Sometimes he'd yell, "Toots! Toots! You gotta see this!" We'd joke back and forth, and he'd say, "Sch-h-h-t, Tootie, you're not right in the head." We'd both laugh, and he'd get so tickled. My heart soared during those moments.

At the end of a day, our family always kissed one another goodnight. In pure Dad fashion, he'd offer us girls his chin, and my sisters, Mom, and I would hug each other and call out our "night-nights." You might consider us the Kentucky redneck version of *The Waltons*. (Yes, we swam in the cow trough during blazing hot summers!) But there was a lot more to our family's television show.

Dad was no Pa, and I was no Mary Ellen. But John-Boy? That was my sister Diana. She and I were the rough-and-tumble farm girls, while Sherri stayed in the house with Mom, moisturizing with Oil of Olay and warning us of impending wrinkles. (I should have listened to her. Today she is the only one of us girls without a face lined like a Tennessee road map.)

Something else that distinguished our family from the Walton clan was a single event in 1979. It changed each of us and sent us down a path of trial and survival. I was fifteen the year it happened—the year my dad's abandonment tore apart our home and our hearts.

Broken Apart

Dad in a casual, offhanded way asked Mom for a divorce at the kitchen table one afternoon after he came back from a week of working on the railroad. At first he confessed infidelity—which my mom indicated that she could live with—but then Dad took a sledgehammer to her heart and to our family. After twenty-five years of marriage, he was leaving Mom for another woman.

By this time my sisters were married and out of the house I was seventeen. Dad never talked directly to any of us girls about his decision. As I recall, a week or so later, I was sitting on our worn paisley couch, watching him carry out his clothes and other belongings as Mom followed him, begging him to stay and sobbing inconsolably.

Dad took a sledgehammer to her heart and to our family. After twenty-five years of marriage, he was leaving Mom for another woman.

Dad seemed oblivious to my mother's suffering. He'd come home now and then to get a few things, as if he didn't want to leave the past completely behind. And every time he visited, a fresh wound opened in my mom's heart. She would wail and beg him to stay.

Shortly after the divorce, Dad took me away for the weekend. The excitement of being alone with him and having the chance to talk about our family quickly evaporated when he revealed that we'd be staying in a cramped trailer with his new girlfriend, Irma.

It was not a great weekend.

Rage and hurt feelings consumed me. I confronted Irma, and in turn she said mean, coldhearted words about my mom, such as if she weren't so overweight, perhaps she could have kept her man. Who knew life could be so harsh!

My world, postdivorce, came to an all-confusing, all-consuming, agonizing standstill. For those of you who've faced your parents' divorce as a child or adolescent, you know what I mean.

Some people report that their parents' divorce experiences contain a modicum of sanity, civility, and sensitivity. I experienced the opposite of any healthfulness or sanity. My mother, clearly broken by Dad's revelation, went through shock, denial, and heavy grief, and then she sank into a deep fog of depression. Her nervous breakdown lasted more than a year.

Mental health care was not on many folks' minds back then, at least in our small town. My best friend at the time, Lona, recently reminded me that I slipped my mother a Quaalude in the midst of one of her particularly bad episodes.

I came to despise my mother's weakness. I remember wanting her to buck up and be the adult. I needed her to be strong and stable, or at least just to show some anger toward my dad. She literally hung on his shirt every time he came home, crying and begging him to stay. I thought, *Why would Dad want to come back to a doormat?* The extent of her humiliation made me cringe.

Certainly I loved Mom more than life itself, but I, too, was hurting inside and angry. I was Daddy's girl, and he was gone. Her misery only added to my own. I began to spend more and more time away from home, away from the chaos.

Ravaged Inside

In the South, everybody is a Christian. It's not an act or decision. Getting baptized is just something you do. But in the wake of Mom's breakdown, a few strong Christians, including a pastor and his wife, came to visit and check on her. They encouraged her to commit her life to Jesus. From then on she was never without her Bible. At the time, it disgusted me. It turned my stomach to see her on her knees in prayer. I preferred Dad's rebellion, which translated to strength. I rebelled too.

Reckless, self-destructive behavior became my new normal at the age of seventeen and remained so for many years to come. My daily routine included sporadic attendance at school, smoking weed, drinking, and having sex with whomever, whenever. And I got in trouble—a lot of trouble—at Lincoln County High School. Fortunately, or at least I thought so at the time, my sister Diana was the recipient of phone calls from the principal's office and police station. Somehow with both of my parents out of the picture, and with Diana married and stable, she became an official go-to adult. I don't recall the details, but I'm sure I got her on the first-to-call list with some fast-talking and deception.

A year after the divorce, we lost our family home, and Mom was forced to live in a motel room. I chose to live out of my car, which meant storing my stuff in The Bomb and sleeping at my friends' homes. Hence, the twin mattress strapped to the car with a garden hose.

God's favor followed me. He knew my future. He knew that like my mom, someday I would belong to Him.

Even then, God's favor followed me. He knew my future. He knew that like my mom, someday I would belong to Him. And I'm certain my anger, pain, and destructiveness grieved Him. My saving grace at the time came from Lona's folks, Daddy Dub and Ida May Brogle. They were strong believers and loved me unconditionally. Their door was always open, and I was always walking through it. Daddy Dub will tell you, "That's because we lost the house keys!" I mooched many a meal at the Brogle home and hunkered down with Lona several nights a week. Their family became a safe, sane haven for me, and of all of their "adopted" kids, I'm their favorite, or so they say!

Lona recently told me that she remembers our going out on the town just after high school graduation. As we pulled out of the driveway, Daddy Dub came over to the window to reinforce the unspoken rule that we needed to be home by midnight. This is Lona's recollection:

There I was grumbling under my breath as we drove away. After all, I was almost eighteen years old and paying for my own car. I didn't understand why I couldn't stay out as late as I wanted. But then I looked over at you, and there were tears streaming down your face, and you said, "I love it when your dad tells us when we have to be home. I wish my dad even knew where I was." I always think about you when I'm telling my kids to do something they don't want to do.

My dad, who once worked by my side doing farm chores, who took us on Sunday outings for ice cream, and who laughed with me over shows like *Carol Burnett* went through periods when he wouldn't talk to or even acknowledge any of us girls. He would ignore us even if we drove past him on the road or saw him at the market. Perhaps avoiding us was also his way of avoiding the pain and devastation he had caused our family.

Forgiving Dad

I am now in my late forties, and some memories of my teenage years remain a blur. At the same time, it's as if they took place only yesterday. I still suffer from the choices I made, especially the promiscuity I engaged in well into my twenties.

Now I'm a Christian women's leader who personally knows the ins and outs of sexually transmitted diseases, and at the same time, I am uniquely qualified to talk about grace—and throw in a good measure of forgiveness, too.

Yet it took me years to get to this place. And it didn't come without sacrifice or action on my part. The playwright Eugene O'Neill wrote, "Man is born broken. He lives by mending. The grace of God is glue."[1] The Lord in His infinite mercy knew my future, and His grace sustained me as a child, a teen, and a young woman. But it would take time before I'd turn toward Him, my Abba Father, and begin the long process of mending.

Let me tell you, forgiveness does *not* mean forgetting. Nor does it mean refusing to face reality. In fact, if you don't consciously choose to make amends, the offense or hurt continues to rear its ugly head.

This hit home for me a few years after Tommy and I married. At that point, I had yet to really acknowledge or deal with the impact of my parents' divorce or my dad's subsequent desertion. Oh sure, little things would come up from time to time, but it wasn't until one incident brought me face-to face with my past that I saw what I needed to do.

Let me tell you, forgiveness does not mean forgetting. Nor does it mean refusing to face reality.

It happened on a summer afternoon, when Tommy was playing horse with our twin three-year-old daughters. The girls were screaming with laughter, and Tommy wore a permanent smile on his face. It was a sight that should warm the heart of any mom—but not mine. After some wringing my hands in worry and anger, I put a stop to the merriment. I sent the girls into our fenced backyard to play. Tommy asked me what the problem was, and through tears I told him I didn't exactly know. I just knew that I didn't want the girls to get too attached to him; I didn't want their hearts broken by what I foresaw as his inevitable abandonment of us. It was then that I desperately knew I needed to make peace with my past. My first act was to forgive my dad.

I come from the "just do it" school of forgiveness. To forgive my dad, I had to set aside—often—my emotions. It required a deliberate act that went beyond myself and what I am capable of.

I'm daily reminded of my dad's incarceration and the pain he's caused our family. My sisters and I are on the receiving end of the often selfish and controlling litany of demands in his letters from prison. He rarely, if ever, communicates with us in the way our little-girl hearts still crave. There are many times when we all have to remove ourselves from his life for our own sanity and for that of our families. At other times, I receive letters that elicit a strong mixture of laughter and sadness, like the other day when I received one with nothing but a joke. Do you want to hear it?

Tootie,

This old drunk named Lonnie-A was walking down near Fishing Creek Road. He'd had too much wine. They were having a baptizing in the creek. The preacher waved Lonnie-A over and said, "Come into the water so you can meet the Lord." So the old drunk said, "I'll try it." The preacher held him under for ten seconds and then pulled him up and said, "Did you meet the Lord?" The old drunk said no. So the preacher dunked him for another fifteen seconds, and when Lonnie-A came up, the preacher said, "Did you meet the Lord?" Again, no. So this time he held him under for a full thirty seconds, and when the old drunk came up for air, the preacher said, "Did you meet Him this time?" And Lonnie-A said, "No. But are you sure this is where He fell in at?"

Love,

Dad

My dad and I share a love for humor and the ability to talk our way in and out of any mess. I love him—and I have feelings of hatred. Forgiveness is ongoing. So practically, how did I—and how do I—"just do it"? I spent time reading various authors, such as R. T. Kendall, on forgiveness. I asked a lot of questions, and I, of course, prayed. I prayed for Dad, too, that he'd learn to love God with great passion and that God would use someone, somewhere in that prison, through acts of compassion and kindness, to break through the hard shell surrounding Dad's heart. I also prayed that the power of Scripture, which "is living and active, [and] sharper than any double-edged sword . . . dividing soul and spirit, joints and marrow" (Hebrews 4:12), would find its way into my father's prison cell.

Consistent prayer has helped break through my anger. I have also meditated on God's promises in Scripture, specifically on what He says about the nature of human relationships and His plan for them. Plus I've read books about others who have walked the journey of forgiveness. All these things—prayer, scriptures, and reading—have helped change my heart over time.

Consistent prayer has helped break through my anger.

Finally, I am haunted by the Bible verse, "In prayer there is a connection between what God does and what you do. You can't get forgiveness from God, for instance, without also forgiving others. If you refuse to do your part, you cut yourself off from God's part" (Matthew 6:14, MSG). I take this scripture seriously. Some days I ask for forgiveness hourly for my shortcomings and the ways I fail God and others. In this way I also experience great freedom by not having the static of broken relationships, hurt words, and wrong thoughts or actions hanging over my head. My dad is certainly part of this picture. When something reminds me of how he's hurt our family, I usually stew awhile, but then I pray and ask God to help me forgive and to remind me all over again of the brokenness that stalks all of us.

Forgiving Dad is a process I'm committed to for the rest of my life. It has given me peace about my past and hope for my future. And most important, it has allowed me to trust my husband and God's plan for our family.

FORGIVENESS CREPES

This fragile, yet fantastic recipe will require several tries before getting it right. By perfecting this recipe, you'll also be learning oodles and oodles about perseverance and forgiving yourself.

Ingredients
- 2 cups milk
- 2 eggs
- 1¹/₂ cups all-purpose flour
- pinch salt
- 1 stick (4 ounces) unsalted butter, melted
- orange butter sauce—recipe follows
- 1 tablespoon butter to brush the skillet or crepe pan
- vanilla ice creaml

Directions
1. Preheat oven to 350 degrees F.
2. Add milk and eggs to blender and combine. Add the flour ¹/₂ a cup at a time, blending after each addition to ensure there are no lumps. Add pinch of salt and melted butter; then blend for 30 seconds until you achieve a smooth, silky consistency. Set aside in refrigerator for at least 30 minutes to rest. While it rests, make the orange butter sauce.
3. Dip a piece of kitchen paper in butter and grease a small frying pan. Ladle a spoonful of batter into the pan. With a flick of the wrist, swivel the pan in order to get a nice even covering all over. A good crepe should be paper-thin. Cook on high heat and flip it over when you see the edge turning golden brown. Remove crepes from pan, fold in half, and press into a muffin tray to form little cup shapes. Bake in hot oven for 10 to

12 minutes until slightly crispy and brown around edges. The middle should remain spongy and light.

ORANGE BUTTER SAUCE

Ingredients
- 2 sticks ($^1/_2$ pound) unsalted butter
- 1 cup granulated sugar
- 1 cup freshly squeezed orange juice
- $^1/_2$ lemon, juiced
- 1 teaspoon orange zest
- 1 big splash orange flavoring or liqueur

Directions
1. Combine butter, sugar, citrus juices, and zest to a small saucepan and cook on low heat for about 10 minutes until it caramelizes. It should be a golden color. Remove from heat, add orange flavoring, and return to heat. Continue to whisk and reduce until syrupy—about 10 minutes. When done, set to the side.
2. To assemble, place crepe "cup" in center of plate and place a scoop of vanilla ice cream in the cup. Drizzle with orange butter sauce.

Life or Death

This day I call the heavens and the earth as witnesses against
you that I have set before you life and death, blessings and curses.
Now choose life, so that you and your children may live and that
you may love the LORD your God, listen to his voice, and hold fast
to him.

—DEUTERONOMY 30:19–20

As a senior in high school, I wormed my way into all of the club pictures, though I wasn't a member of anything but the un-official stoners' club. In our senior yearbook I was voted Most Mischievous, Class Flirt, and Class Clown. That pretty much sums up my academic experience.

I hurt and therefore I hurt others in my longing for love. I didn't real-ize it at the time, but I was using others to fill my void. It didn't matter to my selfish needs. My life in high school was damaging on many levels. I became enmeshed in bad behaviors and abusive relationships. I still regret the pain—physically and emotionally.

After graduation, my friend Lona and I took jobs as desk clerks at a nearby hotel. I continued my nomadic lifestyle, but at least now I was gainfully employed. And at the front desk I fell head over heels in love with Michael, a fellow clerk whose dad owned the hotel. Michael was handsome and funny, and we clicked almost immediately. We became inseparable.

Michael's presence, as with all the guys I dated, helped me feel less empty inside. A big part of my promiscuity involved my aversion to being alone at night with my thoughts and demons. If I wasn't snuggling up to my friends at their families' homes, I yearned to be held by a man. I hated sleeping alone.

Michael wasn't the greatest influence on my burgeoning drug habit. Most of our money was channeled into partying supplies, especially cocaine. But we were in love. During our relationship of about five years, Michael and I discussed marriage. Unfortunately, I hailed from the other side of the tracks, and his mother opposed the relationship. If Michael married me, Mommy said he'd not only lose his country-club status but also his inheritance.

Then a fateful phone call plunged my life into deeper despair. The year was 1982, and I was nineteen years old. I was sitting in my friend Janet's living room when the phone rang.

I took the phone. Three words from another friend, a lab tech at a free clinic, struck fear in my heart. "It's positive, Yvette."

Pregnancy. A paralyzing prospect. I could marry Michael, but he'd have to defy his mom and lose his blue-blooded lifestyle. Not promising. I still had nowhere permanent to live and very little money. And how would we be able to care for a baby all the while nursing our drug habits? Questions like this one ran through my brain for days.

Michael, of course, was devastated by the news as well. We decided to keep it all simple and quiet. In the end, it seemed like a no-brainer: We chose the route of abortion.

I felt okay about my decision until the afternoon before the date. According to Lona, she tried to talk me out of it. I had completely blocked out this conversation until recently. This is Lona's account of that awful day:

> You called me on a Tuesday night. We were getting ready for church,
> and you were crying. You said, "Lona, I have an abortion scheduled for
> tomorrow, and I need you to talk me out of it." So I told Dad that I
> couldn't go to church, and that you really needed our prayers. I ended

up telling him and my momma so they could pray for you. I was hugely against abortion, and I came armed with all sorts of material and brochures. And I sat down with you and said, "Tootie, you cry if a puppy dies; you'll never be able to live with yourself if you kill a baby."

I stayed with you for four hours. Michael was so angry that I was pressuring you to have the baby and filling your head with doubts. He said that you guys weren't ready to be parents. I talked to you about adoption and going to live at a home for unwed mothers. I talked to you until I was blue in the face! When I left, I knew that you were going to have the abortion. I was absolutely sick.

The next day you called to say that you made it through okay. And I never judged you for it. Neither did my parents. We loved and treated you the same. I never talked about it. But you brought it up from time to time over the years and volunteered that it was for the best and that it didn't bother you. You brought it up so much that I knew it was killing you inside. I remember that you called years later. You were crying and said, "Lona, you were right all along. I know God forgives me, but I can't forgive myself." We talked a long time that night.

I've blocked out most of the memories of my abortion. I recall the nurse giving me a Valium to take off the edge. I stayed awake throughout the procedure. I heard a loud vacuum sound and thought, *There it goes.*

Michael waited for me in the clinic lobby. We spent the night in a hotel. He brought me chicken noodle soup and Sprite to soothe the vomiting. And then we slept. The next day we drove to his brother's house, and I smoked a joint to help numb the pain and to push down the reality of what we had just done—what *I* had just done!

If I was spiraling downward before, now I was heading straight for hell on earth. I dove into nonstop partying and other emotionally numbing activities. Being in a mind-altered state helped stave off the growing storm of personal issues gathering over my head.

Escape from Kentucky

Life was crumbling for me in Kentucky. I still had no permanent place to live; I still loved a man who wouldn't marry me; I still had those emotional and spiritual issues following me. They stalked me. It seemed like the perfect time to make my escape.

Kids like me rarely left our small town. Most, like my two sisters, married young, birthed their children, and died in Kentucky. But I had to get out. My brother-in-law Chug graciously paid for my flight to Colorado Springs to visit my cousin. Toward the end of my stay, we made a bet: If I could find a job within three days, I'd stay and become her roommate.

I landed a job on day one at a clothing store in the Citadel mall. I worked in the women's clothing department as a sales assistant. I also met a guy named Frank there, and he and I became the closest of platonic friends. He was like the brother I never had!

Frank worked in the men's department, and he fueled the party girl in me. We did virtually everything together. One evening after work, his car broke down, and he called his brother Tommy to come help. As we sat waiting, I turned to Frank and said, "I didn't know you had an older brother." And then Tommy pulled up.

The first time I laid eyes on him I thought, *Who is this hunk of man? And why have you been keeping him from me, Frank?*

After we fixed the vehicle, we invited Tommy to join us for a play at the Air Force Academy. He agreed, and we spent the evening talking and getting to know each other. We both fell hard.

Tommy and I eventually moved in together.

One morning, several months into our relationship, I felt nauseated. *Oh no, here we go again*, I thought. I went to the doctor and took the test, and sure enough, I was pregnant. I broke the news to Tommy. He didn't believe that we were ready for a family. I was still fairly unreliable as a girlfriend, and we had our problems as a couple. Basically, I had cheated on him weeks earlier, and he was still unsure whether he wanted to spend the rest of his life with me. Tommy urged me to consider abortion. In fact, he said if I wanted to have the baby, I should move back to Kentucky. He didn't want any part of it.

So I made the appointment. But I couldn't go through with it. Two weeks later, I made another. This time I got a bit further: I was in a hospital gown, my feet in stirrups, mulling over my options. I honestly didn't think I could survive another abortion—but I also couldn't have the baby alone.

I began to sweat. I felt trapped. I needed air. I fled the room and the clinic, still in the open-backed gown. I sat in my car for a while. Then I drove away; I couldn't even go back for my clothes. *I can't get rid of this baby*, I thought.

I began to sweat. I felt trapped. I needed air. I fled the room and the clinic, still in the open-backed gown.

I broke the news to Tommy the next day, and he was silent.

I made plans to return to Kentucky. I had enough cash and a place to live lined up. I woke up the next morning to find a note on my door. The note was a proposal. Tommy asked me to marry him. He wanted the baby. He wanted our relationship to work. He said he'd be there to support me. I still have the note! Pregnant to high heaven, I walked down the aisle with Tommy . . . and five months later, the twins, (yes, twins!) Lee and Lauren, were born.

God blessed me with these two miracle babies in spite of my two scheduled abortion appointments! Grace, indeed. My life was about to change for the better.

Walking in Others' Shoes

There's a verse in the Bible where Jesus says, "I tell you, her sins, which are many, are forgiven—for she loved much" (Luke 7:47, esv). This truth is living, breathing reality in my life! The transgressions I committed in my lifetime are staggering, but it's given me a grateful spirit and a deep love for God. How can I throw stones at anyone? Seriously, I look at my past and wonder why I am allowed to have the wonderful children that I don't deserve. Why am I allowed to have a marriage to my best friend? And why do I get to speak to thousands of women from a platform of grace?

It's simple. Because God regularly gives the deserved action an undeserved response!

Through counseling, forgiveness, and tackling the issues that led to my rebellion and teenage depravity, I have learned to see life through God's eyes.

Rarely a day goes by that I don't think about the baby that Michael and I conceived. He would be a little older than my other children; he would be making his way in the world. While my actions will always cause me grief, I have learned to forgive myself as God has surely forgiven me.

While it's true that abortion "stops a beating heart," it also dulls, numbs, and deadens the mother's emotions.

While it's true that abortion "stops a beating heart," it also dulls, numbs, and deadens the mother's emotions. I don't think there's any way around this process: If a woman has an abortion, she simply must develop an emotional barrier for survival. A mother must learn to shield her heart from getting too close, from feeling.

Over the years I've served as a spokesperson for abstinence and pro-life causes. I communicate a number of messages concerning these issues, but there are certain concepts that hit close to home. Not only do you cheat yourself by not remaining pure, but you also cheat your future mate. How I wish I could have given Tommy my purity. I robbed him not only of physical purity but also of emotional purity. I gave of myself freely to many others without ever realizing that my body and my heart were being used.

In using sex to fill the voids and longings in my heart, I was setting myself up for hurts that will never go away this side of heaven. Have I forgotten? No. Am I forgiven? Absolutely!

Postscript: Even though Frank lives in Seattle, Washington, we're still like brother and sister. He accepted my and Tommy's life of faith but wanted nothing to do with it for years. Yet Tommy, ever the evangelist and encourager, persistently witnessed to Frank. And last year, twenty-two years after we first met, Frank began a relationship with his Savior and Lord. He is now one of the most on-fire Christians I know!

SLOW COOKER CHICKEN AND CORN CHOWDER

Sometimes life is just too tough to labor intensively in the kitchen. This recipe is an easy one to make but tastes as if it took you all day.

Ingredients
- 6 boneless, skinless chicken thighs, breasts, or tenders cut into 1-inch cubes
- 3 large new potatoes, peeled, cut into 1-inch cubes

- 3 carrots, chopped
- 3 celery stalks, chopped
- 1 red bell pepper, seeded, chopped
- 1 leek, cleaned, chopped, if desired (optional)
- $1/3$ cup chopped onion
- 3 cups frozen corn
- 1 can (4.5 ounces) chopped green chiles
- 1 package (3 ounces) cream cheese, cut into cubes
- 2 cups chicken broth
- 2 cups milk
- 1 cup cooking sherry
- 3 tablespoons butter
- 1 tablespoon sugar
- $1/2$ cup heavy cream
- 2 tablespoons cornstarch
- salt and pepper to taste
- 1 pound crumbled, cooked bacon for garnish
- $1/2$ cup chopped fresh parsley for garnish

Directions

1. In slow cooker, mix all ingredients except whipping cream, cornstarch, salt and pepper, bacon, and parsley.
2. Cover; cook on high heat about 4 hours, or on low heat 8 hours.
3. In small bowl, beat whipping cream and cornstarch with whisk until smooth. Stir into mixture in slow cooker. Cover; cook 15 minutes longer.
4. Season chowder with salt and pepper to taste. Garnish individual bowls of chowder with bacon and parsley.

four

Tastes Like Chocolate;
Feels Like Flannel

*I do not at all understand the mystery of grace—only that it
meets us where we are and does not leave us where it found
us. It can be received gladly or grudgingly, in big gulps or tiny
tastes, like a deer at the salt. I gobbled it, licked it, held it down
between my little hooves.*

—ANNE LAMOTT, *Traveling Mercies*

*I*n parts of Kentucky, some persons are unaware that the war between the North and the South ended nearly 150 years ago. I kid you not. The average American wouldn't know about this age-old Southern grudge, unless, of course, he or she dropped a loved one from New York into blue-collar eastern Kentucky. Enter my husband, Tommy.

When the girls were a year old and our son, Buck, was a newborn, my brother-in-law graciously offered Tommy a job reseeding land after coal had been extracted (the official term is *hydroseeding*). Tommy was eager for gainful employment to support our growing family, and I jumped at the chance to be near my sisters, my mom, and my best girlfriends.

So we packed up and moved from Colorado Springs to the hinterlands of Kentucky, where one might see a scene straight from the 1972 thriller *Deliverance*. (To this day, the sound of banjos makes Tommy think the infamous "they" are after him.)

We relocated to an area that is spitting distance from Butcher Hollow (pronounced "Holler"), famous for being the home of Loretta Lynn. We were proud to be in the *Coal Miner's Daughter's* neck of the woods, a mining community steeped in generations of tradition.

I enjoyed my first summer back. I have to admit, I spent the majority of time by Sherri's pool, immersing myself in the joys of motherhood and happy hour every day at four.

Tommy, on the other hand, was suffering from culture shock. He was on the receiving end of harassment, name calling, and slurs, such as "damn Yankee." Tommy was a foreign man in a foreign land.

Still, he put his best foot forward, getting up every morning and working hard. But the adjustment proved too difficult. Clinical depression—which would become a lifelong battle for Tommy—set in after six months or so. His brand of blues translated to staying in bed all weekend with the blinds closed.

I, on the other hand, had an adequate support system. I relished having my family around. I had help with the babies, and my sisters and I laughed, played, and cooked up a storm for every holiday. There was something wonderful about being back in Kentucky. Author Donald Miller says, "Everybody has to leave, everybody has to leave their home and come back so they can love it again for all new reasons."[1] This was definitely true in my case.

My next-door neighbor was a Christian woman named Ranie. Our children were about the same age, and we regularly walked our strollers around the same neighborhood loop.

Ranie knew I wasn't a Christian. I still smoked pot and drank and had a vocabulary that would have made a grizzled truck driver cringe. But she loved me anyway.

I used a string of expletives at the end of a story one afternoon, and Ranie told me that my mouth would one day be used to bring God glory. I yawned: She was always slipping this kind of thing into the course of conversation.

Little did I know that Ranie and her merry band of Christian friends were praying for me to commit my life to Christ. Prayer is a powerful medium—and my mom also had been faithfully engaging in it on my behalf. I really didn't stand a chance.

Little did I know that Ranie and her merry band of Christian friends were praying for me to commit my life to Christ.

One day while I was making lunch for my babies, a grease fire started on the stove. I tried to put it out, but only managed to spread the fire and smoke. By the time I called the fire department, flames were shooting up from all corners of the kitchen.

I got the kids out of the house.

When the firefighters pulled up, I was standing on my front lawn in my house robe, with bare feet, my hair askew, and a posse of runny-nosed children around me. The only thing missing was a lit cigarette dangling from the side of my mouth. I looked true Kentucky country.

And I had totaled the kitchen.

Looking Back, Moving Forward

On August 25, 1990, I saddled Tommy with the kids for the weekend. Depressed or not, he'd have to take over our parenting duties; I was determined to go to my ten-year high school reunion.

There was a dinner planned for the first evening, and then a dance. And all my closest friends were planning to stay at a local hotel. I had the whole shebang planned out—for two nights we'd take a break from adult responsibilities and relive the glory days of high school.

So the evening started off fine for me, though I missed the kids.

As the party got going, I didn't want to drink (an unusual happening in and of itself). Everyone around me was drunk or getting there, and I just wanted to show off pictures of my babies and talk about being a mom.

Sadly, I knew that no one would remember my kids because of their inebriated state. As I looked around the room, I didn't want to face the results of drinking or the morning after when no one would remember what had happened the evening before.

I desperately missed my family. So I arose at the crack of dawn and left.

Perhaps it was exhaustion, I don't know, but I started crying almost immediately after I got into the car. In a blur of tears, I missed my highway exit by miles. I kept picturing friends slurring drunk and talking about their kids. And I knew that was me. I was no better or worse. And I knew that I was not the wife and mom I wanted to be. I longed for what my friend Ranie had going for her.

So I prayed out loud to God for the first time. I said, "I will give You a year and trade my crap-life for what You have for me."

Ranie was a devoted, loving mother and wife and lived a pure, clean life. I felt dirty—and I wanted to be clean. I didn't want to smell like an ashtray and day-old liquor. I longed for forgiveness. I was so sick of my life, sick and exhausted of trying to fill the many holes in my heart with things that only brought pain.

So I prayed out loud to God for the first time. I said, "I will give You a year and trade my crap-life for what You have for me. I'll give up drugs, alcohol, cursing, and my filthy life. I'll give it all up if You show me how

Your way is better than my own. Help me to be clean and to be a better wife to Tommy, and a good momma to my babies."

Yes, I promised God a year—I thought, *Hey, let's not get crazy here*—just a year. I can do anything for a year!

I arrived home, and Tommy was surprised. I was scheduled to be away for the whole weekend.

Guess who wasn't surprised by my early arrival? Ranie. She knocked on my door with a Bible in hand. She had been up all night praying for me, and she knew in her heart that I'd be home early, having made a decision to follow Christ. What an amazing revelation! I'm still blown away by her faith.

In the wee morning hours of August 26, 1990, the course of my life was changed forever. I was finally in the family of God.

So This Is What It's All About

Within a week a troop of women, armed and ready for battle, came out of the woodwork. They needed a second baseman for their softball team. They sought an extra body for their Bible study.

I didn't know it at the time, but this was a serious covert operation. Their mission? To nurture and encourage the former cussing sailor and new believer. In the days to come, wise, mature, loving Christian women surrounded me and helped build my new faith. They loved me up—and most important, they were real.

They also offered great advice. They warned me not to shove a salt-shaker of religiosity down Tommy's throat—not to gag him on this new thing. (I did give Tommy a Bible tract explaining the way to finding salvation in Christ.) They encouraged me to let my actions shine through, and to pray without ceasing that he, too, would come into relationship with Jesus. Soon there were a couple of cookouts scheduled, and the men appeared on the scene. We had a ready-made community!

These women cared for me. And they made Christianity attractive and palatable. Christianity wasn't about a series of dos and don'ts, big hair, weeping televangelists, and judgments; it was about responding in obedience and relationship to a loving God who sacrificed His Son on the cross. It was about exchanging my filthy lifestyle for a life of forgiveness.

I also learned that Christians prayed often, not just at the beginning and end of meals. What a huge revelation! They modeled faith by turning to God in every circumstance, especially to find answers for life's challenges. Turning to God meant praying or meditating on different scriptures in the Bible.

Christianity wasn't about a series of dos and don'ts, big hair, weeping televangelists, and judgments.

They also celebrated my wacky personality. They'd say, "Yvette, you are so creatively, fearfully, and wonderfully made. God handpicked you to be the mother of these kids. And He delights in you."

I had finally found what I was looking for in life—what I was desperately needing! A loving and faithful Father to fill my emptiness and deepest needs.

A New West

I only wish the same had been true of Tommy's world. In late 1990, his situation was not improving. He confided that if he didn't leave Kentucky soon, he'd probably end up taking his life. "Then we have to leave now," I remember saying.

I borrowed a thousand bucks from my dad—which quite possibly came through dishonest means—and we rented a moving truck. With pennies to our name, no place to live, and no job, we moved back to Colorado Springs.

Reluctantly, we relocated to Tommy's parents' home. I loved my in-laws, but I knew our growing family might be a lot for them to handle long-term. Without much of a choice, but grateful for a roof over our heads, the five of us hunkered together on prisonlike cots in their basement.

They didn't want a high heating bill, so the basement in January didn't rise above fifty degrees. Hell had frozen over, and it was only a matter of time before one of us woke up iced to the steel bed springs.

Tommy got a landscaping job fairly quickly. I clung to my green *Life Application Bible* and the sweet honey taste of new faith, but only Jesus kept me from lashing out at my mother-in-law. But our situation did come to a breaking point.

One night before bedtime I turned to Tommy and said, "Tomorrow morning is when I kill your mother." To my relief, he said, "You'll have to beat me to the punch." I continued, "I don't care if we have to sleep on the streets of Nevada Avenue, we have to get out of here." The next day we found a two-bedroom apartment, and I was the happiest girl in the USA.

I should note that we are close to Tommy's family. We love them all!

I eagerly continued to pursue my new faith, mainly at the Heart of the Springs Church. My pastor was a great spiritual teacher, and I found a group of friends who helped keep me accountable in the weak areas of my life. The girls were four and Buck was three when I applied for a night-shift job answering the phones at a nearby ministry called Focus on the Family. It was August 1991.

Three notables from my interview process stand out: One, I took the typing test three separate times and failed. They finally said, "Never mind." Two, I referred to the president of the organization, Dr. James

Dobson, as just Dobson repeatedly before the interviewer brusquely corrected me. Three, a cyst on my ovary burst during my final interview at Focus. I was doubled over in pain. I couldn't walk or breathe, so I asked the interviewer to leave the room while I curled up in a fetal position on the floor in cold, clammy agony.

A cyst on my ovary burst during my final interview at Focus. I was doubled over in pain. I couldn't walk or breathe.

Nonetheless, I could talk up a good storm, and I loved Jesus. In spite of my rough introduction to Focus, I was hired.

I continued to grow spiritually, and I prayed fervently for Tommy to enter into a relationship with Jesus. I still heeded the advice of Ranie and her comrades. I loved Tommy and tried hard to model the virtues of faith, including patience, kindness, hope, joy, and especially love. By now, he knew that this guy Jesus wasn't just one of my passing fads. Yet he still didn't ask questions or express any desire to join the kids and me at church.

Despair set in at times. I really wanted him to know all that I experienced, and to be part of our family's spiritual journey. I wanted us to be on the same page.

Then it happened. Three years after I prayed the life-changing prayer, Tommy came home from a turkey hunt all smiles. *Did he bag our Sunday feast?* I wondered. *And will I have to pluck it?*

It was Mother's Day, and he handed me a bouquet of flowers and a card. I opened the envelope, and the tract I had given him shortly after I became a Christian dropped out. He had kept it in his wallet for three years.

Could it be? I sensed something had changed in him, though I expressed a healthy skepticism.

"Why today?" I asked.

"I can't be the husband I need to be or the father I need to be without Christ," Tommy replied. "I've seen the change it has made for you, and I want that too."

We rejoiced! It remains *the* greatest Mother's Day ever!

From that time forward, Tommy never turned back. He is one of the most faithful, integrity-filled, Jesus-loving men I know. I am a fortunate woman!

Stepping-Stones

I came out of a salty background. And by the sheer grace of God, I spent a year with women who poured their wisdom into me. Most beneficial, I observed how they loved their husbands and children. They modeled grace, forgiveness, and joy even in the toughest of circumstances.

God fulfilled my desire to be changed from the inside out that first year, and I strive to be a better wife, mom, daughter, and friend, and confidant. At the same time, my old friends will tell you that I'm still the same Yvette. God didn't change my personality or the unique essence of who I am. I'm still crazy—He now uses all of it for His glory.

The grace I received, the love I was shown, and the passion God has instilled in me for the gospel, I am able to freely give to others. And He brings those in need along. Constantly.

Serving God at Focus on the Family for twenty years was the greatest privilege. During that time I was promoted to supervisor, manager, director, vice president, and eventually senior vice president. And all along the way, I had frequent opportunities to share my story of redemption. It happened in public restrooms, at restaurants, in airports, and at all sorts of events. God arranged miraculous appointments with people who longed for a listening ear, grace, and a bit of wisdom.

It usually began with some stranger spilling his or her guts.

I remember flying back from one of our Renewing the Heart conferences where I, along with others, spent an entire weekend speaking into the lives of and praying for thousands of women. At the time, I was serving as the Vice President of Women's Ministries.

**The passion God has instilled in me
for the gospel I am able to freely give
to others. And He brings those in
need along. Constantly.**

I buckled into my middle seat on the plane and tried not to make eye contact with anyone. I was thoroughly exhausted and looked forward to a long nap. However, the lady sitting next to me piped up and asked where I was headed. I answered but didn't follow up with a similar question. I. Wanted. Sleep.

She began to tell me, unprovoked, that she was going to meet her lover. That she was planning to cheat on her husband with someone who was also married. Odd to blurt this kind of information out to a perfect stranger, don't you think? But at that point, I knew this was a divine appointment—God tapping me on the shoulder, if you will—and I prepared to crane my neck to the right for the next three hours.

This ill-kempt woman needed help.

She shared her broken heart with me. Over the course of the flight, I told her that God had so much more in store for her and her marriage. I cried with her over the bind she'd gotten herself into. I mentioned my work with Focus and the resources and counseling we could provide to get her family through this rough patch.

She asked what she could do; she was already in flight! I told her to exit the plane after landing, turn around, get back on another flight, and put her marriage back together. The plane landed, and we hugged. And we stayed in touch. Thankfully, she and her husband chose to do the hard work to make things work.

I had a similar encounter while visiting the Broadmoor hotel in Colorado Springs over Mother's Day weekend. My husband treated my preteen daughters and me to a girls' night out. We played, swam, and ate well, pretending to be tourists in our own town.

While I was lounging by the pool, the girls chatted with a man and a woman who were also swimming. After a half hour or so, the man got out of the pool and came over to let me know how proud I should be of my daughters and their boldness to share their faith and relationship with Jesus Christ. I thanked him and resolved to enjoy my spa-like atmosphere.

After a few moments of thinking that I must be the best mom on the planet, the woman who was with the gentleman in the pool came over to talk with me. Half expecting the same accolades from her, I sat up proudly to talk. This however was not her conversation. Her words were of heartache, sadness, and disappointment in her life and with her own children.

She had a broken marriage and serious questions about God's plan for her life. My heart broke as she and I talked for an hour or so. She was actually away from her children on this Mother's Day weekend because she couldn't bear the rejection of staying home and not being appreciated or called or sent a card.

We talked and prayed and cried together. As she got up to leave, she humbled me by calling me a "stepping-stone" in her weekend. She said that the Lord had placed me there by that pool at the Broadmoor just for her.

She recalled as a child going down to the creek in back of her house and needing to get to the other side. The water was flowing fast and furious, and she had to look for stepping-stones to cross. She gave me a great word picture of how it is to raise the children God has entrusted to us. She said it's like a roaring river that we have to cross. We may get wet. We may not end up exactly straight across the river from where we began; or we may be soaked by the time we get to the other side. But the point is *to get to the other side with everyone intact!*

The only way to cross is by placing our feet on the stepping-stones. Christ is a stepping-stone. The Bible and its promises are stepping-stones. And the people, resources, and encouragement He places along our path are stepping-stones.

**Christ is a stepping-stone. The Bible and
its promises are stepping-stones.**

My new friend at the pool helped me remember that this journey is a daily one and often arduous. Even though I had a very proud moment over my daughters' faith, I was reminded that each day is a new one with its challenges.

I could tell you dozens of stories of how God has allowed me to be used as a stepping-stone. Every aspect of my story—from my troubles with Dad, to my abortion, to my wayward ways—is useable if I allow the Lord to use it.

I've learned that in a world of need, people need us to be authentic, and they need us to listen, see where they hurt, and cry with them. They desperately need the grace that was shown to me when *I* was undone. Grace: I certainly didn't earn it or deserve it, yet it was given to me freely. And when it arrives on the scene, it's so familiar and deep that it tastes like chocolate and feels like flannel.

KENTUCKY DERBY PIE

Feeling blue? Bake this chocolate-and-pecan concoction, invite some friends over to share it, and soon you'll be feeling like a winner.

Ingredients
- 1 unbaked 9-inch pie shell (I use one with a graham-cracker crust)
- ½ cup (1 stick) butter
- 1 cup sugar
- 2 eggs
- 1 teaspoon vanilla
- ½ cup flour
- 1 cup semi-sweet chocolate chips
- 1 cup pecan halves (I chop or break most in small pieces)

Directions
1. Preheat oven to 350 degrees F.
2. Cream butter, sugar, and eggs. Add vanilla.
3. Gradually mix in flour.
4. Stir in chocolate chip and pecans.
5. Pour into unbaked pie shell. Place on baking sheet.
6 Bake for 30–45 minutes, until top is nicely browned. Remove from oven.
7. Let set at least 2 hours before serving.

five

Mishaps, Funny People, and Mistaken Identities

She could never be a saint, but she thought she could be a martyr if they killed her quick.
—FLANNERY O'CONNOR, "A Temple of the Holy Ghost"

As a tot I hung on the hip of my oldest sister, Diana, like a baby chimpanzee. She carried me around while she milked cows, worked in the fields, and did household chores. The three of us sisters were left to our own devices while Mom worked full-time and Dad was away on the railroad.

I ran wild on our farm and, according to Diana, "made a habit of climbing furniture like a monkey." To this day I'm still persecuted by my sisters for a perceived lack of work ethic in my childhood. Diana always says that any time there was work to do—dishes, dusting, laundry—I was in the bathroom. She still wants to know what I was doing in there all that time.

I, of course, have a different recollection, which was backed up during a recent visit to see my father in prison. "A hard worker," he said of both Diana and me. My sister Sherri is still determined to write her own book and set the record straight.

Our weekends were filled with farm chores. Sometimes Dad would bellow, "Get me some cigarettes, Tootie!" We didn't cross Dad, and we had better not be caught with our hair in a towel when he needed something.

But even then I'd look for the fun in a negative situation. I'd hop on our riding lawnmower and head to the store to get him smokes, which was no short distance away. Or better yet, I'd ride our horse, Star, bareback.

I'm still persecuted by my sisters for a perceived lack of work ethic in my childhood.

Star was a working mare, big and black, with Clydesdale feet and a gigantic rear. I'd pick up pop bottles scattered in the ditches along the way and return them to the store for nickels. The trip was redeemed if I scored enough change to buy a drink and maybe a candy bar. And this is where Star proved to be infinitely valuable. On hot summer days, my spindly, sweaty legs gripped her massive sides while she hobbled along, giving me an elevated view of the ditch lines for maximum bottle pickup. I'd slide down her side, bag the bottle, and then hoist myself up from a fencepost.

Summers and School Days

In the summer we sisters spent our days working on 4-H projects, caring for our farm animals, and having sleepovers at our grandparents'. When I was very young, my job was to sleep with Grandma Frankie Greer. I remember her snores shaking the walls. Then in the morning I was charged with emptying her pee pot. (Think bedpans for the outhouse crowd.) I distinctly recall Grandma Frankie wringing the necks of chickens and making a one-pot soup in the fireplace, along with cathead biscuits (a technique of pinching dough, not cats). To this day I'm easily lulled into a nostalgic haze at the smell of biscuits baking.

Another job was to deliver groceries from my grandparents' store to several of our neighbors. Two neighbors stood out: Clara and Emma, a mother-and-adult-daughter duo. They lived on a hill in a big house covered in moss and surrounded by weeds and overgrown trees. The daughter, Clara, was what we then called "mentally ill" and spent her days playing cards and chain-smoking on her back porch. My sisters pushed me through the front door to deliver their order and do all the talking—I was (and am now) always the talker.

Clara and Emma also owned a pet monkey. On Halloween the monkey would sit on Clara's shoulder and hand us unwrapped marshmallows. Everybody in our small town came out of the woodwork on fright night. Many of the adults in the community, including my dad, played late-night pranks: Farm animals were painted like zebras, and trees were cut down and laid across roadways.

Every fall, my sisters and I rode the bus to school. We got up at the crack of dawn and traveled dirt roads along the creek. I'd fight sleep and a queasy stomach as the yellow behemoth belched gray smoke and unsuccessfully navigated potholes the size of swimming pools. The afternoon ride home seemed more horrific when the heat and humidity bore down on us, and dust and dirt blew into the metal-framed, slide-lock windows—you know, the ones you'd struggle to open with your thumbs, only to have them come crashing down like guillotines.

My friend Lona recently reminded me of our high school study-hall teacher, Miss Bell. She had a problem with her voice and emitted a grating, high-pitched tone when she spoke. One day I was talking during class—which was a common occurrence—but on this afternoon, Miss Bell tried to put a stop to it.

Miss Bell started to raise her voice higher and higher, saying, "Denise, Denise, hush your talking!" (Denise is my aunt.) And I had no idea that Miss Bell was talking to me. So I kept on talking. And she kept getting more agitated. At this point, everyone in the room was quiet—except me, of course—and they probably wondered, *Who is Miss Bell talking about?* And then Miss Bell stormed over to my desk, smacked me across the head, and said, "I'm talking to you, Denise!" And I turned to her rather defiantly and said, "I'm not Denise; I'm Yvette."

Then Miss Bell said, "Don't you play tricks on me. I know who you are." Everyone burst out laughing. I got kicked out of study hall and had to sit in the principal's office for the rest of the semester. But, according to Lona, I didn't seem to mind, and I made the best of it. I even nabbed a book of hall passes.

Menstruation in Midair

My colorful Kentucky background, coupled with my personality, set me up for a lifetime of unusual happenings. And I've learned that the best way to approach them is not through embarrassment or shame—though in retrospect, I do feel bad about the Miss Bell incident. Instead I laugh, find the humor and irony, and make every effort not to take life so seriously.

Along those lines, I've had at least three notable off-color incidents on airplanes. And no, none of them have anything to do with the Mile High Club. Get your mind out of the gutter, people! One of these events, in particular, is every woman's nightmare. When you get a bit older, time and gravity alter your internal workings . . . You know the score, ladies. One moment you're sipping a foamy cappuccino and poring over your journal. And the next moment you're a crazed woman battering down the coffee-shop restroom door.

This one time I was traveling to California with a few work colleagues when catastrophe struck. It was an early Tuesday morning, and we were at Denver International Airport. It was a short trip, in and out for two meetings and one speaking engagement. And it would become the first and last time I'd check my bag—actually it was a small rolling carry-on that I checked at the gate. It held my standard stack of reading material, pajamas, toiletries, and a fancy speaking-engagement kind of outfit.

We boarded the plane without incident and took our seats. My coworkers and I sat in different rows. I was in the middle seat, sitting next to a kindly older gentleman and a woman immersed in an issue of *Family Circle* magazine. I took out my book and settled in for the two-hour jaunt to Southern California.

As we were taking off, my stomach felt queasy, and my back started to ache. I attributed it to turbulence. (Denver International Airport is literally a mile high in elevation, with nearby mountains, and the strong wind currents often make for a bumpy ride.) The rumbling inside my inner being continued past takeoff though, and I suspected something was amiss. Then it happened: As the plane leveled out, my water broke—only I wasn't pregnant, and it wasn't water. I was suddenly "in the Levitical way." I was flooding—with no advance warning.

As the plane leveled out, my water broke—only I wasn't pregnant, and it wasn't water.

So there I sat with the seat-belt sign still illuminated and the lady to my right and the gentleman to my left completely unaware of my turmoil. I knew I had to get to the restroom—and soon. So I violated every FAA regulation and climbed over my seatmate into the aisle. I shuffled my way down the aisle and mumbled a few cursory words to the still-strapped-in flight attendants as I entered the tiny bathroom.

So what does one do in this situation? In my experience, not much when you're at 30,000 feet and ascending into the heavens. I tried to wash out my khaki pants, but to no avail. My efforts resulted only in getting blood on my blouse. For a good hour I pushed the steel button atop the sink and emitted tiny bursts of pink industrial foamy soap. I scrubbed with all my might, shredding an entire forest of cheap paper towels in the process.

Finally, all hope was lost. I couldn't return to my seat. My clothes were permanently ruined. I tossed them into the airliner trash, and rolled my eyes, thinking, "Why do these kinds of things always happen to me?" Yet, the truth is, we all have accidents of this stripe—life is full of them!

So I launched Plan B. Yes, a second but seemingly questionable option emerged. I opened the door a crack, poked my head out, and waved down a flight attendant. I explained the situation, and as I looked up and down her five-foot-four-inch, size-four figure—and thought about my size-twelve, five-foot-ten-inch frame—I cautiously asked the flight attendant if she had any extra clothes I could borrow. Hey, beggars can't be choosers!

I can only describe her reaction as gracious and sympathetic. We women have to be there for one another, right? She said, "I'll be right back." I closed the bathroom door, settled back into what had begun to feel like home base after such a lengthy time, and waited.

I cautiously asked the flight attendant if she had any extra clothes I could borrow. Hey, beggars can't be choosers!

When she returned she handed me leggings and a midriff shirt. I looked at her and smiled. I wasn't sure *one* of my thighs would fit in *both* legs put together. How in the world was I going to climb into these pants? And the half shirt! Needless to say, I asked for a blanket to cover my behind and midsection. Let the freak show begin.

I returned to my seat wearing high-heel shoes, leggings that came up to my calves, and a small, blue fleece blanket wrapped around my midsection. I took my seat. The lady looked up from her reading material and asked if everything was okay. After all, I had been missing in action for nearly an hour and a half—and I looked weird. I gave her a pleasant but obligatory nod.

The plane landed without any additional incident. And I was on a mission: Walmart or bust. I grabbed my carry-on, thanked the flight attendant profusely, and exited the Jetway.

I had to connect with my colleagues. Dave was the first to approach. He looked understandably puzzled and exclaimed, "Yeah, Yvette . . . Hey, that's not the outfit you were wearing when we boarded, is it?" After briefly explaining the situation and facing my other coworkers, we made a beeline to the store so I could purchase a pair of slacks, a sweatshirt, and some necessary female articles.

After I returned to Colorado, I washed and sent the clothes back to the flight attendant along with a hefty Starbucks gift card. She saved my life! I also had a good belly-laughing, tears-streaming-out-of-the-eyes story to tell my girlfriends.

Sarah Laughed Too

Sarah and Abraham from the Old Testament in the Bible also had a tale for their friends and neighbors. Sarah had been painfully without children her entire marriage. No fertility treatments in 2000 BC! But God surprised them. An angel came down and informed the couple that at ages ninety and one hundred, they were pregnant, and they'd have a boy and name him Isaac.

Frederick Buechner says in *Telling the Truth: The Gospel as Tragedy, Comedy, and Fairy Tale* that upon hearing the news, "Abraham laughed until he fell on his face," and another account says, "Sarah was the one who did it." Buechner says, "They are laughing because laughing is better than crying and maybe not even all that different. They are laughing at God and with God, and they are laughing at themselves too because laughter has that in common with weeping. No matter what the immediate occasion is of either your laughter or your tears, the object of both ends up being yourself and your own life."[1]

So where does laughter emerge from at a time of tragedy? "It comes from as deep a place as tears come from, and in a way it comes from the same place," says Buechner. "As much as tears do, it comes out of the darkness of the world where God is of all missing persons the most missed, except that it comes not as an ally of darkness but as its adversary, not as a symptom of darkness but it's antidote."[2]

Airplane mishaps are certainly not on the scale of tragedy, but they do represent bumps in the road that can bring us down, send us into a panic, or give us the option to deal with the situation with winsomeness and grace. Whether riding on the back of giant working mare while picking up pop bottles, sitting in the principal's office, or dealing with less-than-appealing situations, I have always tried to see the humor and irony.

Bumps in the road . . . can bring us down, send us into a panic, or give us the option to deal with the situation with winsomeness and grace.

I take to heart scriptures such as "The joy of the LORD is [my] strength" (Nehemiah 8:10). Or "Count it all joy, my brothers, when you meet trials of various kinds, for you know that the testing of your faith produces steadfastness. And let steadfastness have its full effect, that you may be perfect and complete, lacking in nothing" (James 1:2–4, ESV). God wants us to experience joy. He is an all-encompassing God of love, justice, truth, and power, but I suspect He also delights in a good joke and the quirks of our humanness.

ROBERTA'S HALLOWEEN POPCORN BALLS

Roberta lived just up the road from Clara and Emma's house where, the monkey gave us marshmallows for trick or treat. We loved escaping the monkey and running to Roberta's house.

Ingredients
- 1 cup melted margarine
- $^1/_2$ cup light corn syrup
- 2 cups brown sugar
- 1 teaspoon salt
- 6 to 7 cups popped corn

Directions
1. In a medium saucepan, combine margarine, corn syrup, brown sugar, and salt. Melt all this together.
2. Fold in the popcorn.
3. Spread the entire mixture onto a baking sheet.
4. Bake for one hour at 225 degrees F. Stir every 15 minutes.
5. After cooking, either form into balls or let cool.
6. Store in airtight containers.
7. Roberta placed the popcorn balls in a plastic sandwich bag. She tied a pretty ribbon around the top.

six

Blown Away

That light we see is burning in my hall.
How far that little candle throws his beams!
So shines a good deed in a naughty world.

—Portia in *Merchant of Venice* by William Shakespeare

*I*t all started when I agreed to attend a gathering in Chicago called the Chicagoland Christian Women's Conference (CCWC). I arrived in the Windy City on a Thursday afternoon and checked into my hotel at around three o'clock. The first meeting on my agenda, scheduled for 4:30 PM, was with the CCWC board members. They had invited me to be a fly on the wall as they prayed for the upcoming conference and tended to other board business.

After grabbing my room key and getting the lay of the land, I prepared for my typical "I'm away from my husband and kids" nesting routine. One of my favorite things about traveling for work is being able to have a hotel room all to myself, with my *own* bed, multiple pillows, remote control, bathroom, and so on. This visit to Chicago was no exception. I took great pleasure in placing my things into the drawers and hanging my clothes just so on the hangers. After unpacking my suitcase, I set up the bathroom with my hot rollers, an assortment of makeup, hair accessories, my toothbrush, and dental floss. Everything was in a neat and tidy row.

I planned to use any available free time on this particular trip to catch up on writing letters to my dad and other neglected family members. I had even bought two new packages of flowery note cards to help inspire me. I placed the cards on the desk in my room, alongside supplies for other projects I hoped to complete. These included all of my devotions and writings from the past few years, along with a big folder of journal entries that I intended to use as a resource for writing new teachings for upcoming engagements. As if these materials weren't enough, I had also included Kathy Troccoli's book *Am I Not Still God?* and a Focus on the Family manuscript to proofread. (Stay with me—this exhaustive list will be significant later in the story.)

By the time I arranged my room, it was time to head down to the board meeting. What a wonderful group of ladies! The CCWC women welcomed me to their gathering as if I were part of the family. We had a great discussion about how Focus could help meet the needs of the African American community in general and women in particular.

The board meeting adjourned at 8:20 that evening. I hadn't eaten all day, so I stopped at the hotel restaurant to look over the menu. I enjoy reading while I eat, and because I had a year's worth of material in my room, I decided to head upstairs to grab a book before ordering something. I was staying in room 502, so I pushed the elevator button for the fifth floor. But when the doors opened and I started walking down the hall, I sensed that something was wrong. Nothing in the area looked familiar to me. So I went back to the elevator to make sure I was in the right place. After confirming that I was, in fact, on the fifth floor, I made my way toward room 502 with an uneasy feeling in my gut.

At this point I need to offer a brief explanation of fire-safety measures for those of you who might not have stayed in a large burning hotel recently. If there is a fire, the affected area will automatically be sealed off by a complex system of impregnable steel doors.

These metal barriers isolate the flames and prevent them from spreading. It was into this environment that I entered when I got off the elevator—an imposing labyrinth of metal that looked nothing like a hotel hallway.

At that moment, three men—one of whom was carrying a fire

extinguisher—came whizzing around the corner. "Stand back!" one of them yelled when he saw me, and then the three of them yanked back the metal doors and prepared to run—you guessed it—straight into room 502! I asked one of the men what had happened, and the firefighter answered that someone must have left a cigarette burning. My heart sank at his words.

The firefighter answered that someone must have left a cigarette burning. My heart sank at his words. I knew what had caused the fire.

I knew what had caused the fire.

While arranging my nest earlier in the day, I had lit a small votive candle (another part of my routine whenever I check into a hotel) to help freshen the air and set a mood of calm and relaxation.

The man, clearly growing suspicious, asked, "Is this your room?"

I must confess that I was sorely tempted to answer no, bolt to the lobby, and leave the hotel! But as I stood there in complete disbelief, I weakly answered, "Yes, this is my room"—and then looked for a big planter or some kind of receptacle in which I could throw up. My stomach curled into knots, and my knees went weak. I couldn't breathe, and all I could think was *Oh no—I did this!*

After a few moments, the men finally emerged and said that it was safe for me to enter the room. One of them kept asking me if I was all right, and for good reason. I must have been as white as an uncharred hotel bed sheet. I timidly entered the room, expecting the worst.

I was not disappointed.

The towels hanging in the bathroom—which a few hours earlier had been crisp and white—were now covered in ugly black soot. Ditto for my hot rollers, toothbrush, and accessories. I turned the corner to find that the desk, which previously held my numerous important papers and documents, was now *gone*! The lamp, the files, the note cards, and even the desktop itself had been reduced to ashes. Everything else in the room, including the beds and all of my clothes in the closet, was covered with soot.

As I continued to look around the room, I realized that the sliding balcony doors were open, and that an icy cold Chicago wind was coming in and blowing ashes everywhere.

I was in a terrible state of panic, and the only thing I kept thinking was *Oh no—I did this!*

Jeff, the rooms manager (and the one who kept asking me if I was okay), was also a Chicago volunteer fireman. He tried to comfort me by noting how much worse it could have been.

"In another ten minutes, we would have had to evacuate the hotel," he offered.

I imagined all of the hotel guests (senior citizens, parents with small children, and everyone else) standing outside in the twenty-three-degree Chicago night while the building burned in front of them. In ten more minutes that nightmare would have been a reality. Jeff wasn't helping me feel any less sick.

I explained to Jeff that while I had lit a candle earlier, I was *certain* that I had leaned over and blown it out before leaving my room for the board meeting. I could distinctly remember blowing the candle out before walking out that door. There was an intense smell of vanilla and wax, a smoldering wick, and a trail of smoky vapor rising into the air.

Jeff, a short, stocky man with kind eyes and a thick Chicago accent, nodded knowingly and explained that when the door to a hotel room is shut, it creates a vacuum that results in a rush of air in the interior. The men surmised that when I shut the door, the resultant rush of air either relit the candle or lifted one of the many papers on the desk causing it to touch the smoldering wick.

Once the mystery had been solved, a bellhop proceeded to gather all my soot-covered belongings and put them into garbage bags. He had already secured a key for a new room. Jeff tried to ease my mind as much as possible. "Go get a good night's sleep," he said, "and we'll talk tomorrow." Before departing he also asked, "Can I get you anything? Coffee? Some dinner? A good stiff drink?"

As delicately as possible, I explained that I just needed a private bathroom so that I could throw up! (I realize this is the second chapter that mentions violent stomach issues. This is my life, friends!)

Have you ever felt complete helplessness? Complete disbelief? I was so sick to my stomach that I could barely move.

I entered my new room, stinky garbage bags in hand, and sat down. Have you ever felt complete helplessness? Complete disbelief? I was so sick to my stomach that I could barely move. I sat there in the darkness and recalled the times I left my house in the past, only to experience discomfort at the thought that I might have left the iron turned on. Had I experienced that same uncertainty earlier on this particular day, I could have gone back to check the candle!

I sat there with nothing but my bag of soot. I had no idea what consequences would await me when I met with the hotel personnel the next day. My perspective was gloomy, to say the least.

A spouse has the ability to either make or break a traumatic situation for his or her mate. I called my husband to break the grim news. The conversation began casually enough. He told me all about his day, the kids' day, and so on. Then it was my turn. I mustered my courage, swallowed my pride, and said, "Honey, I have something horrible to tell you . . ."

Thankfully, Tommy brought some needed levity to the conversation. After I recounted my tale of woe, he laughed and said, "Only *you* could torch a room at a hotel and not burn down the whole building!"

I expected to get the "what were you thinking?" speech. But instead he simply encouraged me to look on the bright side. He said, "Hey, baby, it's just a room! No one was hurt. You're not hurt. It's under control—and God must have a whole new message for you if all of your devotional materials were burned up!"

After talking to Tommy, I could breathe again. What a perspective! I realized that despite the craziness of my situation, there really could be a purpose for everything that had transpired.

What should we do in those moments of complete disbelief and total helplessness? We have to attempt, at some point in the game, to put them into perspective. And this doesn't happen by wringing our hands and letting our hearts dictate our reactions! Sometimes this means talking through the situation with a spouse or close friend or crying out to God.

How can this turn around for good? Show me, God.

For me that night, it meant starting a new journal. I sat down and wrote, "Thank You, God, for all things, both good and bad. I am scared and can't breathe with this smell all around and this soot taste in my mouth, but I trust You, God. I'm worried about the cost of this nightmare, but I trust You. Please make this lump in my throat go away. Help me trust You! Thank You for Tommy and how he helps me see things with a new perspective. Show me everything new. Help me to learn from this situation. How can this turn around for good? Show me, God."

Earlier in the evening, I had lamented the fact that my possessions had been turned to ashes. Now I needed to put what had transpired into *perspective*. I thought about Isaiah 44:20, which reads, "He feeds on ashes, a deceived heart has turned him aside. And he cannot deliver his soul, nor say, 'Is there not a lie in my right hand?'" (NKJV). How often in our lives do we feed on ashes with a deceived heart?

I realized that the ashes blowing around my first room that night represented the "yuck," the everyday weaknesses and sin in my life. So often, we feed on this yuck rather than look for God and accept the beauty that He can bring out of any situation. And yet, He promises in Isaiah 61:3 that He will bestow "a crown of beauty instead of ashes, the oil of gladness instead of mourning, and a garment of praise instead of a spirit of despair."

As I drifted off to sleep, I prayed, "Please make the smell go away from my one existing outfit. Help me as I talk with the hotel manager tomorrow about the cost of the damages, and finally, please show me why this happened!"

Grace to the Rescue

The next morning I met with a man who is a good friend of our ministry, Jeffrey Wright from Urban Ministries. I had tried so hard all morning before our meeting to get the smoky smell out of my outfit, but it didn't take Jeffrey long to realize that something—or rather *someone*—was carrying a strong odor. I finally asked him straight out, "Do you smell me?"

We both laughed, and he asked if I'd been chain-smoking. I shared what had taken place the night before. Jeffrey then said, "The Lord must have a whole new message for you to allow this!" I got goose bumps as I remembered that Tommy had said exactly the same thing.

On Saturday morning I met with the manager of the hotel to review the damage estimate. My heart sank as he handed me a bill for $3,660.72. I had purchased two beds, a lamp, towels (bath, hand, and wash), some wallpaper and carpeting, and several other hotel room accessories. Tears ran down my face, and I told him that I needed to call my husband and my insurance company to find out what to do next.

As I walked back to my room, I began to feel sick again. My mind raced. How am I going to explain this to everyone back at Focus? At least I have the resources to legally leave the building, thanks to my corporate credit card.

Later that evening, Jeff phoned me and asked if he and another manager could meet with me. The two men met me in the lobby, and I got the feeling they were chatting with me for a few moments to ensure I was mentally stable following the fire trauma. I guess I seemed sane enough, because Jeff said he had some news.

The big boss, as he put it, had decided to waive the cost of *all* the damages, including my laundry incidentals! The big boss asked only that I promise one thing—"Make sure that the next time you're in Chicago, you come back and stay with us!"

I couldn't believe what I was hearing. In fact, I was shocked. I stammered, "How . . . why?"

Jeff offered no further explanation other than the big boss had made the decision. I leaped from my seat to give both men a hug. I was overwhelmed by this remarkable demonstration of grace.

In the joy of the moment, I took the opportunity to tell them that my big boss was the *ultimate* Big Boss—the God of the universe!

Now, I didn't give a powerful, come-to-Jesus-style message, and our meeting didn't end in a tearful altar call, but I was able to compare the hotel's gracious actions to the *definitive* act of selflessness and sacrifice: Jesus' death on the cross for our sins. Just as God had sent His Son to cover our sins, He had used the kindness of these two managers and their big boss to help cover my unfortunate candle mishap!

For a few moments, those two gentlemen were able to witness the joy of someone to whom grace had been given. And I think they were able to grasp the idea that the grace they had extended me paled in comparison to the grace God extended to humankind when He sacrificed His only Son on our behalf.

Would a conversation of this nature have taken place if I had not started an inferno in my hotel room on Thursday night? Of course not. I would never have crossed paths with any of the hotel managers had I not inadvertently created a crisis. If the weekend had gone according to *my* plan, I would have attended the CCWC meetings and filled my free time with note writing and reading under the glow of a single votive candle. Then on that final Saturday night, rather than talking with two strangers about concepts such as grace and eternity, I would have been packing my suitcase and organizing my possessions for the flight home. On Sunday I would have rushed off to the airport, having been blessed by the CCWC conference, but having had no other interaction with anyone in the hotel. Obviously, God had other plans for me. All He had to do was allow a fire to get my attention!

Beauty or Ashes

Thinking about that candle incident still makes my heart race. And while I still nest in hotel rooms, I no longer play with matches.

I know that whether my life's happenings are beautiful or ashy or somewhere in between, they have been prescreened by God.

My life is nothing compared with Job in the Bible. God allowed Satan to "sift" this man and take everything, including his children. Poor Job. I always feel sorry for him. God and the Devil had an entire conversation behind his back. Behind his back! It makes me want to cry "foul!" And yet, when I get into a challenging situation, I try to remind myself that the tragedy in this man's life went through God's filter first.

I don't always succeed at this remember-the-sifting exercise, but I know that whether my life's happenings are beautiful or ashy or somewhere in between, they have been prescreened by God. And this is the God who knew me in the womb, who knows all of my comings and goings, and who knows the number of my days. This perspective brings me hope in the darkest or the fieriest of situations.

The Chicago debacle taught me that I can't do much with the ashes in my life, but I can determine my response. And I can ask the Holy Spirit and friends around me to remind me of God's promise that He will ultimately turn them into beauty. I'm still learning to trust the Lord's exchange program. Mourning for dancing, sadness for joy, ashes for beauty? I'll take it!

CHARRED CORN-AVOCADO SALSA AND CRAB SANDWICH

Charred hotel room, not so good. Charred salsa, delicious.

Ingredients for Corn-Avacado Salsa
- 8 ears corn
- 1 tablespoon salt, dissolved in a large bowl of cold water
- $^1/_2$ cup crème fraîche (or marscapone cheese)
- $^1/_4$ cup chopped fresh cilantro
- 3 ripe avocados, peeled, pitted, and diced
- juice of 2 limes
- 1 serrano chili, grilled, unpeeled, and thinly sliced
- $^1/_2$ small red onion, finely diced

- Tabasco or other hot sauce
- salt and freshly ground pepper

Directions for Corn-Avacado Salsa
1. Preheat grill to medium direct heat.
2. Pull outer husks down corn to the base. Strip away silk from each ear of corn by hand. Fold the husks back into place and tie ends together with kitchen string. Place ears of corn in a large bowl of cold water with salt for 1 hour.
3. Remove corn from the water and shake off any excess water. Place the corn on grill, close cover, and grill until kernels are tender, 15 to 20 minutes, turning every 5 minutes. Let cool slightly. Remove kernels from ears.
4. Put corn kernels, crème fraîche, cilantro, avocados, lime juice, chilies, onion, and hot sauce in a medium bowl and toss gently, breaking up the avocado a bit. Season with salt and pepper.

Ingredients for Crab-Sandwich Mixture
- charred corn and avocado salsa
- 4 soft, sesame-topped hamburger buns, toasted
- 16 ounces crab meat (we use Chicken of the Sea Jumbo Lump Pasteurized Crab Meat)
- 1 red onion, peeled and sliced into $1^1/4$-inch-thick slices
- 1 to 2 limes
- $1/2$ cup mayonnaise, optional
- salt and freshly ground black pepper

Directions
1. Salt and pepper crab meat to taste.
2. Spread some of charred corn and avacado salsa on bottom of humburger buns.

3. Top with 2 tablespoons of crab, some sliced red onions, and a squeeze of lime juice.
4. Spread extra mayo on top bun, if desired.
5. Top sandwiches and serve.

seven

Plowing Cement

*A journey is like marriage. The certain way to be wrong is
to think you control it.*

—JOHN STEINBECK, *Travels with Charley*

I brought baggage into my marriage, and it wasn't Gucci. It was
more like a large assortment of paper sacks. Tommy had baggage
too, although his might have been carried in a lunch box. What's
not in dispute is that we built our marriage on a foundation as unstable
as desert sand.

Here's a sampling of our personal baggage when we tied the knot
some twenty-five years ago.

As I have already mentioned, I cheated on Tommy several months
prior to our nuptials. By the time we made it to the altar, I was four-and-
a-half-months pregnant. (For those of you with inquiring minds—yes,
Tommy is the twins' father!) For the ceremony, the entire wedding party
dressed in outrageous but fondly remembered Hawaiian attire coupled
with bad eighties hair.

Our twin girls were born soon after we married. We lacked health
insurance, money, and adequate housing. We had to put cribs in a walk-in
closet—the *only* closet—in our loft apartment. In fact, it feels as if we've
just recently paid off the hospital bills for the twins' birth.

Of course, this chaos wasn't confined to the months immediately
before and after the wedding. Tommy and I both came from checkered
backgrounds, and our high school years were especially so. You know my

story; Tommy's was only slightly better. He was expelled his senior year for tearing up a football field with his motorcycle. Neither of us had gone to college or pursued any higher education or trade.

Perhaps most significantly, we both hailed from challenging family situations, each with its own set of deep, wounding experiences. Statistically speaking, our marriage was doomed from the beginning. We were ripe for a rousing episode of *Jerry Springer* or *Dr. Phil.*

I hope this doesn't sound cliché or pat in any way, but as the years progressed, a growing, vibrant faith and a strong commitment to the vows we made saved us from a dismal ending. There were days when the only thread connecting us was that we stubbornly agreed that we would not divorce. Both of us knew what we were saved from—a lifetime of bad choices, heartache, and hopelessness—the day we put our trust in Jesus. We were eternally grateful to God for loving us, even in our most depraved state. When we consider our past, this parable from the Bible speaks powerfully to both of us:

> [Jesus said to Simon,] "Two men were in debt to a banker. One owed five hundred silver pieces, the other fifty. Neither of them could pay up, and so the banker canceled both debts. Which of the two would be more grateful?"
>
> Simon answered, "I suppose the one who was forgiven the most."
>
> "That's right," said Jesus.
>
> Then turning to the woman, but speaking to Simon, [Jesus] said, "Do you see this woman? I came to your home; you provided no water for my feet, but she rained tears on my feet and dried them with her hair. You gave me no greeting, but from the time I arrived she hasn't quit kissing my feet. You provided nothing for freshening up, but she soothed my feet with perfume. Impressive, isn't it? She was forgiven many, many sins, and so she is very, very grateful. If the forgiveness is minimal, the gratitude is minimal." (Luke 7:41–47, MSG)

Tommy and I both feel as if we've been forgiven "the most." And we are very, very grateful to God for His mercy.

Focusing on My Family

I attribute many of our marital successes to the wealth of knowledge we gained during my tenure with Focus on the Family. The ministry's mission is to build strong marriages and families, and when Tommy and I started out, we were anything *but* strong.

Tommy and I learned so much from the teachings of experts while I worked at Focus. We've tried to make it a practice to listen intentionally and heed the wisdom given to us. We've made every effort to apply those principles to our relationship. And many invaluable counseling sessions have also helped!

Before I dig deeper into some of our struggles and how we came through, let me put this on the record: I am married to a man who is ever-faithful and who loves and adores me and our kids and grandkids. I can say to you all without hesitation that God has given me my husband as a gift! Tommy is a man of strong conviction and principles, and I've never had to worry about porn, cheating, financial impropriety, or violence. He is—and has been right from the beginning of his conversion—an individual who loves God. He is a man of deep faith.

I am married to a man who is ever-faithful and who loves and adores me and our kids and grandkids.

But oh the lessons we've learned! In the early years of our marriage, we struggled with many issues as a result of not having Christ as our foundation.

For years we've had to climb mountains of adversity to finally reach a plateau of contentment. And there's an excellent chance that more summits await just over the horizon. But the same is true of every marriage, right? Maybe you'll recognize a few of these peaks we've had to scale.

Unmet Financial Expectations

One of the more difficult struggles for me was grappling with unmet expectations. I believe I battled this problem much more than Tommy did. In other words, he always respected me, even with all of my shortcomings, but I did not always exhibit respect toward him.

I often resented having to work, which lead me to disrespect Tommy for not being a better provider. Even though the Lord blessed my career by giving me more responsibility and higher pay, there were times when I felt trapped because of the need for my paycheck. Tommy was (and still is) in real estate, and because of the ups and downs of the housing market, it wasn't an option for me to stay home with the children. I had no choice but to work. On occasion when days got stressful, I wanted to throw in the towel and scream, "I'd rather live on the streets than face another day at work."

The "Suck It Up" School of Health

In addition, Tommy had his fair share of health problems. And they were not the terminal kinds that elicit sympathy, at least from me. They have taken the form of constant morning headaches, backaches, stomachaches, and regular complaints about his weight. I have always had great health and rarely experience the daily things that Tommy suffers. So when I do have the odd day when I don't feel well, I ascribe to the "suck it up" school of health. I'm a "cowboy up" kind of girl.

I have rolled my eyes in response to Tommy's complaints. I have tuned him out and acted generally unsympathetic to his plight. Don't get me wrong; I'm generally a sympathetic person—for other people. I think that having to walk my mother through her breakdown and her general inability to cope with life after her divorce definitely impacted me and my ability to empathize. When Mom was on the couch and unable to function, I heartlessly and ignorantly identified that behavior as a character weakness. There are times when I see Tommy's complaints about his ailments as a character weakness. I hate confessing this, but it's true.

Home Decorating Debacles

Tommy and I have clashed over simple domestic issues as well. He buys and sells houses as his profession. Because we live in those homes, we're sometimes on the move and residing in different neighborhoods. This means that Tommy influences our home décor, which is always geared toward maximum resale value. He's gifted at design and decorating, but he prefers the properties to be decked out like model homes. I tend to decorate with memorabilia, quilts, and things hung up with hot glue and duct tape. He hails from a gene pool that is very organized and generally freakishly clean. Me . . . not so much.

The Letter

I wrote a letter to Tommy a number of years ago in which I callously pointed out each and every one of his faults—another thing I hate admitting. I specifically mentioned what I felt was his lack of affection toward me. Today I realize that what I needed was his love expressed in *my* love language, not his! I needed physical affection, and he gave me kind and thoughtful acts of service. He would shower me with little surprises and sweet affections. He gave me a daily blessing by bringing me coffee in the mornings. And yet those gestures meant little to me. And so I wrote the letter!

I wrote, "The physical side of our relationship is an entire conversation on its own. In short, I feel rejected by the second man I have truly ever loved. First Dad, then you. This equals pain and hurt at the deepest heart level. When the depth goes so deep, it translates into bitterness and anger.

Your body image and your self-esteem have always overridden my needs. This is interpreted that yet again, you mean more to you than I do. Therein lies the theme. You first. Your needs. Mine and the kids' are secondary."

I could have been a lot more tactful in the letter, but the rejection was very real to me. It touched the raw parts of my heart and the unmet needs in the relationship with my dad. Again, through counseling I have been able to sort out my wants, needs, and desires that have to do with Tommy and separate them from the hurts, disappointments, and rejection from my dad.

My focus on Tommy's faults made me completely blind to some of my biggest transgressions.

Thankfully, I did ask Tommy's forgiveness for a number of my flaws and weaknesses at the end of the letter. You could say it was schizophrenic in a way. But looking back, it's clear that my focus on Tommy's faults made me completely blind to some of my biggest transgressions.

Tommy hasn't had it easy in the feeling-appreciated area either. I would sometimes say to him, "I love you" or "I want you," and he would ask, "Why?" As a running joke, I'd answer, "Don't force me to come up with an answer." And he would come back with, "You have to; I'm your husband."

The banter hid some deep pain. Tommy had to question my declarations of love with a "why?" because I often didn't respect him, and so my words of affection seemed as empty as a jack-o'-lantern.

Holding the Mirror High

I focused on all of Tommy's faults in my letter, which was unfair. On May 29, 1987, I knew whom I was marrying, and even though I was pregnant,

I did love Tommy and desperately wanted to be his wife. I also knew we were different.

Tommy and I are polar opposites. The first time we met, he kept me waiting while he ran home to iron his pants before we went out. He's an avid hunter. He doesn't have any interest in the arts or dancing, and he's not particularly sociable. He's most comfortable in an orange hunting cap and coveralls. He'd rather sit in a goose blind under camouflage than at a restaurant with a group of strangers. I am much more of a chameleon of sorts, adjusting to any setting. Introvert meet extrovert.

Though I knew what I was doing when I got married, I was still an emotional mess. I had no idea who the real me was, and I took little responsibility for our troubles. For years I failed to hold up the mirror and scrutinize myself—and boy, howdy, what a sad reflection was in that mirror. Once I got a clear vision of myself, I was able to address my flaws (at least the most glaring blemishes), and our marriage changed for the better.

So what are *my* issues? There are multitudes, friends, but for the sake of keeping this chapter brief, let's stick to the mother lode of them all: my communication style—or, in short, my hateful mouth!

Grandma Thelma left the female Greers a legacy: a double-edged sword. On one edge of the sword was the ability to accomplish tasks quickly and efficiently. That skill set was certainly needed on the farm with the variety of daily chores; Grandma's being well organized and capable was often the difference between eating or starving. The other side of the sword was a bossy personality. Grandma Thelma was a strong-willed, weather-beaten country woman who moved along at a fast, clicking pace. Everything was always in motion. Everything was planned. Everything was accomplished. She gave commands. If Grandma needed flour, she never asked Papaw Walter politely; she barked the order at him.

The women in our family, from sisters to cousins, inherited the controlling tone (or "gift" we like to say). We do joke about it. If you're listening for it, you'll recognize certain undertones such as, "I'm right; you're wrong" and "You better get out of the way 'cause I'm comin' through." It also says, "I don't need your opinion. You're deadweight and holding me back!"

The Greer women have one speed, and it's fast. If you're going to jump into the discussion while we're clicking away, just don't ask a lot of questions. If you do, we'll look at you with a "what?" expression of exasperation!

On the positive side, when you want something done right, ask the Greer girls. We don't sit for long; we get the job done swiftly and completely.

But kindness is often sacrificed in our efficiency. This was the shadow Tommy lived in for years. But in him, I met my match. He would not be controlled. He would not bow down to the Greer legacy of control. Yeah, sure, sometimes he'd completely shut down. But a battle would ensue whenever he stepped up and stepped in.

Things are just peachy when you mix a broken past, a needy person, an enabler, and some codependent tendencies for good measure!

Because I charged in on situations of all kinds, Tommy felt demeaned and disrespected. I didn't seek his input or consultation on many decisions. To be completely honest, his opinion wasn't always of value to me. And this damaged his self-esteem. Therein smoldered repressed anger and frustration on his part—and it built up for years. Things are just peachy when you mix a broken past, a needy person, an enabler, and some codependent tendencies for good measure! I laid myself emotionally bare in many counseling sessions when I admitted that I desperately needed Tommy and his love, but I didn't always respect him.

I first recognized the Greer legacy as a major problem when I heard

Lee and Lauren sounding strangely similar to me. One day when they were talking to Buck and his friends, I heard my tone coming out of their mouths, and it scared me! Here was the next generation of Greer women—confident, arrogant, bold, controlling, clicking away with little patience—in two nice, pretty packages.

My tone was a constant theme in counseling. Another thread was my feeling that Tommy didn't love me. This was due to my unmet expectations that loving me meant allowing me to do things as I want. I want to rule the roost. This all translated to me that Tommy didn't unconditionally embrace the essence of who I was. We wrestled on and off with these issues for years, but the volcano blew on December 27, 2008.

Volcanic Ash and Other Calamities

The heat began when Tommy hired a business coach for a new venture. The man insisted on involving both of us in the decisions, and this meant talking to me once a week by phone. The arrangement seemed okay to me at the time. However, the coach began to share some of his frustrations about my husband, even confirming some of my worst thoughts. While I didn't conspire with him, this man caused great division in our marriage. He seemed to commiserate with me.

In spite of the coaching, Tommy's career ventures began to fail, which caused a tremendous amount of division between us. No surprise, we got into a huge fight. I didn't respond to Tommy's frustrations in a way that was respectful, which further fueled his fears that he would never live up to my expectations.

Tommy exploded and said, "I'm done. I won't be under your thumb any longer. You're not going to disrespect me." And he threw down the gauntlet and asked for a separation.

In the aftermath, I sat in a brown recliner in our living room. I felt nothing but despair and suffocation. I felt trapped by my marriage and my faith and my professional obligations. I felt so trapped that I dug my nails into my arm and drew blood. To this day a scar remains, and it reminds me of the battle that once and for all changed the face of my marriage.

Tommy and I discussed separation the day after the big blowup. We began to talk about who would leave the house and so on. We even told the kids. That was my decision, not his, which set up another heated disagreement.

A lot of tears were shed on December 27 and 28, 2008. But life moved us through the motions, and Tommy and I were scheduled to go out of town on New Year's Eve. Several years earlier we had started a tradition of retreating to a mountain cabin with friends for the holiday weekend. The deposits had been paid, so rather than cancel the trip, we put our separation plans and grief on the back burner.

Before we left I called Mike, our marriage counselor. "We've hit a really, really bad place," I told him. "Please pray for us. He's done. I'm done."

We couldn't get physically apart at the cabin, so it forced us to be a couple in front of other couples. We put our masks on, and we were forced to be civil. Under normal stress levels, we're pretty open with our friends, but the situation still felt way too volatile to bring up in this festive setting.

"Just don't think I'm going to roll over, Tootie. Things are going to change. They have to change, or I'm done."

As notable foodies among our friends, Tommy and I were in charge of cooking flank steak. We worked side by side chopping, peeling, sautéing, tasting, and plating—all the basic cooking activities that force two people to work together. Later we even basked in a multitude of accolades as a team. Our masks were perfectly in place. After we finished eating and playing board games with our friends, we wished everyone a Happy New Year.

"Is this how we're going to start 2009?" I asked in bed that night. We both cried ourselves to sleep over the thought and over the emotional carnage of the past few days.

We both returned home raw and vulnerable. We put our separation plans on hold and ended up in Mike's office in January 2009. As we began the session, Tommy said, "Just don't think I'm going to roll over, Tootie. Things are going to change. They have to change, or I'm done."

The fabric had finally torn. And we had a long way back—and forward. We stayed together in the fight because we believed ours to be a holy marriage, a covenant worth battling for. We believed God would honor all of the blood, sweat, and tears we left on the floor.

Lessons Learned

I'm so thankful that Tommy stood his ground with me and that he loved me enough to work through these trials in our marriage. I realize that many men have too much pride to lay their feelings and vulnerabilities on the table with a counselor. In all humility, Tommy held up a mirror to himself and said, "What do I need to work on?" and "How can I love my wife more fully?" And I had to do the same.

I've also learned through much trial and error that I need to keep the details of my marriage as part of a regular conversation with God. And I've failed to focus on all the positive, amazing attributes that my husband brings to the table: the daily things, the wonderful things. Hey, he picked me up at the airport recently in a new-to-me shiny silver Toyota convertible! I have a thoughtful partner who showers me with surprises. Life isn't all rough!

For such a long time, I had focused on Tommy's shortcomings and not my own. I'm saddened that he had to exist in the shadow of my impossibly high standards for so long. But I wasn't able to appreciate Tommy until I looked at myself in the mirror. When I held it up, I didn't like my reflection. I was selfishly consumed with my own needs and desires.

I was feeding a multiheaded beast of negativity. This realization set me free inside. I began to see my husband through a new filter, and I slowly learned to forgive and to love him, warts and all. What once seemed like mountains suddenly became molehills.

Mantle of Authority

Many people in the Christian faith and those at Focus on the Family believe the "mantle of authority" in a family belongs to the man and is given unconditionally by God. It is provided for spiritual leadership of the home. This doesn't—and shouldn't—strip any of us women of our power, talent, beauty, and influence.

Here's a word picture I often share at speaking engagements: In our marriage I was the strong leader and the more mature Christian at first. I became a believer three years before Tommy did. So one day I looked over in the corner of our home, and there it was, just sitting there: the mantle of authority. Much like football shoulder pads, the mantle could provide power and protection. And since no one else had picked it up, I grabbed it and put it on. And guess what? It fit just fine! I got used to it.

I wore it as I shuffled around the house with my stable income. I wore it when I clicked off my list of things that needed my husband's attention. I even wore it when I prayed for him to step up to the plate and exercise the spiritual leadership in our family and marriage.

God began to answer my prayers for Tommy to step up to leadership. And so naturally Tommy went looking for the mantle. He searched all over the house. Finally, he asked, "Hey, Tootie, have you seen the mantle of authority?" I answered, "Why yes, I have it. Why do you ask?"

That's when the spiritual battle ensued. He couldn't pry my hands off of that mantle! I didn't want to relinquish it. I didn't trust Tommy to wear it even though I had prayed for him to want it. Yet what I had to realize is that I didn't have the authority to take it in the first place! It didn't belong to me.

It's my hope that someday my husband and I will stand before the Lord and hear Him say, "Well done, my good and faithful servants."

The authority was Tommy's. And as his, he could break it, lose it, or complain about its weight—but it was still his to keep. I had to ask for forgiveness. I had to say, "I'm sorry I took it." However, my flesh wanted to say, "Hey, pal, it's your own fault because you weren't wearing it!"

Following our reconciliation, I have regularly asked myself these questions:

- Do I want to *be* right more than I want to *do* right?
- Do I want to breathe life into Tommy more than I want to get even?
- Does Tommy trust me with his heart? Am I a safe harbor for him?
- Do I bring him good, not evil?
- Does this scripture hold true for me? "A wife of noble character who can find? She is worth far more than rubies. Her husband has full confidence in her and lacks nothing of value. She brings him good, not harm, all the days of her life" (Proverbs 31:10–12).
- How is my heart with God at this very moment?

I've learned to own my part in our marriage. I've learned to relinquish unmet expectations—often having to lay them down again and again. I now recognize—though not always immediately!—the difference between molehills and mountains.

I've discovered Tommy's many wonderful contributions to my life, to our family, and to the world. And most important, I make it a daily practice to pray about every detail in our marriage, to lovingly protect it as if I were covering a sleeping baby with a warm blanket.

It has been a battle to achieve contentment within our marriage. I even walk with a metaphorical limp (read the story of Jacob and his wrestling in Genesis 32), and I've earned every wrinkle on my face. A good friend calls this struggle a "holy war for marriage." I know that Tommy and I will still face challenges, but we'll keep battling. I may not learn my lessons quickly, but I eventually get it. And it's my hope that someday my husband and I will stand before the Lord and hear Him say, "Well done, my good and faithful servants" (Matthew 25:21).

MARRIAGE-SAVER FLANK STEAK

This is the meal that staved off Tommy's and my separation on New Year's Eve.

Ingredients for the Steak
- 2 cups red wine
- 1 cup cassis
- $1/4$ cup canola oil
- 3 cloves garlic, minced
- freshly ground black pepper
- 1 (2- to 3-pound) flank steak
- salt

WAYNESBURG, CIRCA 1970—A Greer gathering at the swinging bridge on Fishing Creek

KENTUCKY ROOTS

▲ ABOVE
Cows roaming the fields I ran on as a child.

▲ ABOVE
A family tobacco barn as it stands today in Waynesburg

◄ LEFT
WAYNESBURG, 2011—Me sitting on a cow trough, my childhood "swimming pool"

RIGHT ►
POND RIDGE ROAD, WAYNESBURG, 1970—
From left: Me, Mom, Sherri, Dad, and Diana

GROWING-UP YEARS

COLORADO SPRINGS—Lauren at her fifteenth birthday party. Tommy and I went all out on birthday parties for the kids.

ABOVE ▴
COLORADO SPRINGS, COLORADO, 1987—Our wedding day with Pastor Hornbaker. I am almost five months pregnant.

MAHER MEMORIES

ABOVE ▴
COLORADO SPRINGS—Lee making the traditional Christmas mice for our neighbors

◂ LEFT
COLORADO SPRINGS, 2006— Carmela teaching us how to mak her famous pizza bread.

RIGHT ▸
Me and my handsome husband, 2007

MY WONDERFUL . . .

◂ LEFT
STANFORD, KENTUCKY, 1994—
The Maher kids: Twins Lauren and
Lee are 7; Buck is 6.

COLORADO SPRINGS, COLORADO, 2010—Buck, my studly airman!

Lauren, me, and Lee, 2011

STANFORD, 2006—"Coming out of prison" reunion.
From left: Buck, Dad, Lee, Lauren

ABOVE ▲
Dr. Juli Slattery and me, 2011, having "family" fun on *YOUR FAMILY LIVE!*

ABOVE ▲
WAYNESBURG, 2009—Mom with great-grandson Landon

CRAZY . . .

COLORADO SPRINGS, CHRISTMAS, 2011—The whole Maher family

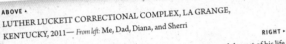

LUTHER LUCKETT CORRECTIONAL COMPLEX, LA GRANGE,
KENTUCKY, 2011— *From left:* Me, Dad, Diana, and Sherri

This dormitory is where Dad will spend the rest of his life.

FAMILY

BOWLING GREEN, KENTUCKY, 2012—*From left:* Diana, Mom, me; and Sherri

ABOVE ▲

Me and my new boss, Brady Boyd, Senior Pastor
of New Life Church in Colorado Springs

LOOKING FORWARD

ABOVE ▲

2011—Me and my little panda, Jaxon. I love being a "nana."

ABOVE ▲

COLORADO SPRINGS, 2011—My punkin! (Landon)

Ingredients for the Chimichurri Sauce
- 1 cup cilantro leaves
- 1 cup flat-leaf parsley leaves
- $1/2$ cup mint leaves
- 4 cloves garlic, roughly chopped
- $3/4$ to 1 cup extra-virgin olive oil
- $1/4$ to $1/3$ cup red wine vinegar
- kosher salt and freshly ground black pepper

Ingredients for the Vidalia Relish
- 3 Vidalia or other sweet onions, skin on, sliced $1/4$-inch thick
- canola oil
- 1 tablespoon Bobby Flay 16 Spice Poultry Rub
- salt and black pepper
- 4 green onions, sliced
- 1 serrano chili, minced with the seeds
- 2 to 3 tablespoons extra-virgin olive oil
- 2 to 3 tablespoons red-wine vinegar

To serve
- 1 baguette
- olive or canola oil
- salt and freshly ground black pepper

Directions for the Steak
1. Mix wine, cassis, garlic, salt, oil, and black pepper in a ceramic or glass dish.
2. Add the steak, turn to coat, and marinate at room temperature 1 hour.
3. Preheat grill to high. Remove steak from marinade and season with salt and more pepper. Grill covered until nicely charred and medium

rare, 3 to 4 minutes per side. Remove from grill and rest 5 to 10 minutes before slicing across the grain.

4. Slice baguette on a diagonal, $^1/_4$-inch thick. Brush with oil, season with salt and pepper, and grill briefly until just starting to crisp. Top each piece with some sauce, a slice or two of steak, more sauce, and some relish.

Directions for the Sauce

1. Pulse herbs and garlic in a food processor until coarsely chopped. Add $^3/_4$ cup oil, $^1/_4$ cup vinegar, and salt and pepper to taste, and pulse to make a soupy vinaigrette—it will look a bit creamy until it settles. Add more oil and/or vinegar if too thick. Set aside.

Directions for the Relish

1. Brush the onions with some canola oil and season with rub, salt, and pepper.
2. Grill onions, turning until charred and soft. Remove from grill and chop coarsely. Chop again with green onions, and then stir together with chile, oil, vinegar, and salt and pepper.

eight

Miracle Whip: The Other White Meat

Poets have been mysteriously silent on the subject of cheese. . . .
It is a short, strong word; it rhymes to "breeze" and "seas" (an
essential point); that it is emphatic in sound is admitted even
by the civilisation of modern cities. For their citizens, with no
apparent intention except emphasis, will often say, "Cheese it!"
or even "Quite the cheese."... But cheese has another quality,
which is also the very soul of song.

—G. K. CHESTERTON, *Alarms and Discursions*

admit, I'm a foodie. I hail from a clan of people who for generations have relished the acts of cooking and eating and the rituals surrounding both. We're canners, bakers, recipe hounds, snobs, rednecks, and sometimes gluttons. For as long as I can remember, food has surrounded celebrations, holidays, and crises, both big and small. It has brought us together as a family and enabled us to maintain and foster traditions.

I should also confess something right from the start: For the majority of my life, I've been happy to let others, including my husband, cook for me while I bellied up to the table. (I like to say that Tommy brought a pasta maker and a garlic press into our marriage, while I came in with a skillet and a well-worn recipe for tuna-and-noodle casserole.) It's only in the last fifteen years that I've discovered the richness of my past and become what I like to think of as the Kentucky version of Julia Child.

The Need

After I became Vice President of Women's Ministries at Focus on the Family, two events converged that changed my relationship with food. First, I began speaking on a variety of issues at our ministry's outreach to college students. As a result, a number of young women sought me out for counsel on dating, marriage, and family. On some fronts, I confidently dispensed advice like cards in a poker game. But on other topics I found myself woefully unprepared.

The young women I talked to were by and large schooled by a fast-food, frozen-food-aisle culture. Sure they knew how to acquire sustenance, but they didn't see—or didn't even know they *should* see—the value of preparing, serving, and eating meals as a family and as a community. But I was like these young girls in one respect: If someone handed me a sack of potatoes, a handful of veggies, and a chicken carcass, I couldn't have made a pot of soup to save my life.

During the same period of time, I met Betty Huizenga, who, after attending culinary school, developed a curriculum for Christian women called *Apples of Gold*. Betty felt led to teach younger women the art of cooking and hospitality. Certainly there has been a renewed interest in food prep with the advent of the Food Network, but when Betty began her ministry fifteen years ago, a whole generation of children was largely ignorant of basic cooking skills.

I traveled to Michigan to see Betty's ministry firsthand. I was blown away by what I encountered. The first thing I noticed was Betty's home; it was the most hospitable, warm environment I'd ever entered. Her kitchen, in particular, took my breath away. It was stocked to the gills with every gadget imaginable, and it smelled like a mixture of cinnamon, yeast, and freshly baked pies. I then watched as Betty employed this impressive arsenal to minister to a group of young women.

She devoted the first hour to a cooking lesson, the second hour to a

Bible study on different concepts related to family and marriage, and the third hour to fellowship and eating what had been prepared during the first hour. My eyes were opened not only to the basics, such as the difference between a dry measuring cup and a liquid cup, but also to the colorful, rich stories she weaved around each part of the meal. I fell in love with the process, the narrative, and of course, the end product.

Food as Tradition

I thought a lot about my own life on the plane ride home. I realized that I was missing the mark by not teaching Lee, Lauren, and Buck how to serve others through cooking (and to be prepared for their future spouses). And I was failing to pass along beloved Kentucky family traditions and recipes. Heck, did I even remember them? I also realized I hadn't done an exemplary job in caring for my husband, Tommy. I owed him something more than fifteen years of tuna-and-noodle casserole.

> I was failing to pass along beloved
> Kentucky family traditions and recipes.
> Heck, did I even remember them?

I got home from Betty's and began to try new recipes. I bought new kitchen gadgets. And I checked out cookbooks from the library. I also sought out mentors who possessed specific cooking and baking skills. One of my favorites became my Italian mother-in-law, Carmela. When I asked her to show me how to prepare old family recipes, such as stuffed cabbage, and pizza bread, it changed the dynamic of our relationship. I stepped into the role of a daughter-in-law that she had only dreamed of—that she didn't even know she missed! For four weeks, she taught me and some of my friends and my family members about Italian food and traditions that otherwise would have died out with her and her siblings. It honored her as much as it did us.

In the end, this period of *Apples of Gold* also helped to enhance our marriage by leaps and bounds. The study is not just about cooking—it's also about loving your husband and developing the virtues described in Titus 2:3–5

I began to mentor Lee, Lauren, their friends, and some of the young women at the ministry in the art of food and the Titus verses. I was shocked to learn that some of them didn't purchase tomatoes because they didn't know what to do with them or that they didn't use green peppers because they weren't sure which parts to cut out and which ones to leave. I showed them a potato peeler and demonstrated how to make stock with scraps of vegetables in the fridge. In the process, we laughed, shared our lives, and grew in relationship. I was able to speak into their hearts in a way that wouldn't have been possible in another setting.

Reflecting on My Own Heritage

Memories emerged as I learned about food, and I began to tell my kids about family traditions and the stories of my childhood. The harvesting and canning of vegetables in big metal washtubs in the heat of a Kentucky summer, the taste of fresh eggs and meat, and the smell of slow-cooked green beans.

Inspired by these memories, we started new traditions. For example, our Kentucky Derby parties became neighborhood-wide events. We'd make mint juleps, sweet tea, chicken salad with grapes on croissants, ham biscuits, corn pudding, and pecan pie. We'd invite all of our friends and neighbors and place our dollar bets just before the Run for the Roses.

To this day my kids can't taste chocolate-covered strawberries without thinking of our popular Derby parties. This gathering gave us opportunities to break down the barriers that kept us from knowing about the lives of people who lived one hundred feet away. We shared the gospel and made life-long friendships. Food and hospitality played a big role in connecting us with others—and tying our memories to the present.

In *Breaking Bread: The Spiritual Significance of Food*, Sara Covin Juengst says, "Eating together is more than just appeasing hunger. It is an activity that includes sharing, learning from one another, and providing for the helpless, a ritual that brings comfort, satisfaction, pleasure, creativity, sustenance, nurture, appreciation, and healing. It satisfies many levels of human needs."[1]

I'm reminded of the Last Supper when Jesus broke bread with His disciples. It was Passover, and they probably served a traditional meal of wine, unleavened bread, lamb, hard-boiled eggs, a nut-apple-spice mix, greens, and bitter herbs—each item symbolizing an important event in Jewish history. Jesus ate with His friends and confidants as a way to bring a sense of oneness, closure, tradition, and community before the dark day of His crucifixion. It must have been a poignant moment for them all, especially Jesus, who knew the difficult trial that lay ahead.

> **Jesus ate with His friends . . . as a way to bring a sense of oneness, closure, tradition, and community before the dark day of His crucifixion.**

The smell and taste of food seals our memories in both good times and bad, sorrow and celebrations. One of my most startling memories concerning food and family involved the joint funeral of my Uncle Shannon (Dad's only brother) and his wife, my Aunt Glenda.

According to some family members, Uncle Shannon was never the same after serving in the Vietnam War. He'd had to go on "nerve pills." So when Aunt Glenda asked for a divorce many years later, it seemed to be the final piece of stress that sent him over the edge. In desperation Uncle Shannon tried to reach out to Dad and a few other family members, but no one grasped the deterioration of his mental state.

I mentioned this event earlier, but here are more details. On a warm May 10, 1990, at the age of fifty-two, Shannon walked into the Waynesburg Elementary School where Glenda worked as a secretary. He shot and killed her. Then he drove to the countryside, and in the same area where generations of us had been baptized and where we swam, played, caught tadpoles and washed cars, he killed himself with a sawed-off shotgun. He left behind a twenty-two-year-old son (who would die from complications resulting from AIDS less than two years later) and a twenty-year-old daughter.

Sherri informed me of the horrible news. This was but one of many calls from her over the years stating, "Tootie, get home!" I had come to expect them. The murder-suicide devastated our family, especially our grandparents. Our joined families had attended school and spent summers together, birthed babies, made ice cream on one another's porches, and shared holiday meals. We had a lifetime of memories. Now we would have a lifetime of shared horror and grief.

When someone dies in the South, a posse of women springs into action. It's an innate, unspoken tradition—and everyone has a role. Some ladies start baking bread, pies, and cakes and letting cinnamon rolls rise. Others make casseroles, beef stews, fried chicken, hams, and deviled eggs.

And you don't just drop off a meal at the home of the grieving family; you go in and make yourself useful. You sit and listen and cry with the stricken family. You look at photo albums, laugh at old stories, and generally pay homage to the dead. In our small town, houses of the grieving would be filled for days with family, friends, and neighbors.

Coming alongside the grieving family meant for some of these women planting themselves at the kitchen sink for hours, washing forks and glasses and filling plates with food for guests. For others it meant unearthing Tupperware and masking tape to write down who brought what kind of dish. Later the same posse of women would write thank-you notes. The job of the griever was to grieve—and to relive the story of their loved one for everyone who came through the door.

After I arrived for Uncle Shannon and Aunt Glenda's funeral, I drove straight to Grandma Thelma and Papaw Walter Greer's home where mountains of food were on display. Obviously, my grandparents were devastated. (One of two sons was dead. Papaw Walter would die a year later with a broken heart. And my dad would be imprisoned several years later, further adding to Grandma's immense sorrow.)

Staying at Grandma Thelma's—even as an adult—meant stacks of pancakes in the morning with peanut butter, crisp bacon, piping hot syrup lovingly made in a cast-iron skillet, and hot coffee. It was as reliable as breathing air. But for the first time in memory, I got up in the morning and didn't see Grandma Thelma. A mixture of grief, anxiety medication, and exhaustion had laid her out.

In one of our family's darkest hours, a group of people used food to meet our basic needs and sit shoulder-to-shoulder with us in our grief.

We were thankful for the women in our community like Fama Patterson, the Women's Missionary Union ladies from Pond Baptist Church, and many others who brought over banana pudding, casseroles, cornbread stuffing, sweet potatoes, greens, macaroni and cheese, fried chicken, soup, cathead biscuits, and berry pies. I recall sitting around the table with my family, absentmindedly noshing on food—picking at crispy chicken and washing it down with sweet tea—and reliving the tragedy both out loud and in our minds. The act of eating brought us together during a crazy-hard experience. In one of our family's darkest hours, a group of people used food to meet our basic needs and sit shoulder-to-shoulder with us in our grief.

More Memories

My most poignant memories outside of childbirth involve food of some sort. As a child I stayed quite often at my friend Mitzi's home. The Caldwells were an exuberant family, and the house was filled with all of the great snacks and choice breakfast cereals.

Our pantry mostly had off-brand imitations of Cheerios and Shredded Wheat, but Mitzi's had Froot Loops and Sugar Pops—the real deal! Freeman, Mitzi's dad, was both a fun and funny character who would wake us girls up at midnight because he didn't want to eat alone. We'd have leftovers or a charred steak with ketchup. Maybe Freeman knew what author Joyce Carol Oates meant when she wrote, "When you live alone, eating carries an element of scorn, mockery. For a meal is a social ritual or it is not a meal, it is just a plate heaped with food."[2]

Greer Family Memories

When we were little, the three of us sisters were charged with setting the table. We were required to eat everything on our plates; nothing was allowed to go to waste. And afterward Mom would place her hand on our bellies; if they felt full enough, she'd give each of us a dime.

I lived on cheese sandwiches in the early years, if Velveeta can be considered cheese! I'd have Velveeta on white bread with Miracle Whip. Papaw Walter would pick me up from school when I got sick—Mom and Dad were working—and Grandma Thelma would fix me Campbell's Chicken Noodle Soup and a cheese sandwich. I ate these sandwiches so often that I didn't always properly dispose of the leftovers. Mom would find half-eaten sandwiches under the bed, behind the couch, and in among the towels in the bathroom. Not a happy sight for her!

Mom was thrifty when it came to food. There wasn't much margin in our family's finances. We always had a gallon of ice cream in the freezer and a can of Hershey's Syrup, because Dad liked it. Our beef, pork, and chicken were butchered in our backyard and stored in a giant freezer. We grew our own vegetables and utilized our potato cellar, where spuds were stacked two-feet high year-round. The potatoes still remaining by the beginning of the next planting season all had green eyes and tiny trees growing out from their dirty brown flesh, and we'd cut them out. Mom would let us eat raw potato slices while she was cooking.

In an age before take-out food, we'd stand around the kitchen on Friday nights and make a Chef Boyardee Pizza Kit. And when we were little and attended church regularly, we'd have potlucks after the service. The food was served from flatbed wagons that hauled hay and tobacco on weekdays. Each family enjoyed their postchurch feast on a blanket spread out on the lawn. On Sundays Mom would also make tuna salad with Miracle Whip, pickle relish, and hard-boiled eggs on white bread. She'd cut the sandwiches into triangles and stack them on top of each other on a platter. We'd wash them down with sweet tea, which is to the South as hot tea is to England.

The three of us girls used to accompany Mom to the grocery store every Saturday afternoon. We could always count on two treats. One, Mom always let us pick our own TV dinner out of the freezer section, a Banquet turkey dinner, complete with a tray divided into little sections and filled with turkey, dressing, mashed potatoes, and peach cobbler. The second treat was a game Mom would initiate with us in the checkout line. We all guessed how much the grocery bill would cost, and the girl who came the closest got to pick out the restaurant where we'd have burgers and fries—usually A&W or Jerry's J-Boy Restaurant, both drive ups.

Sometimes the winner even got to have a milkshake with her lunch. This used to put us over the top!

Greer Holidays

Holidays were especially bountiful. We'd go over to our grandparents' and enjoy a Butterball turkey (just out of the oven, juicy and crisp), thick brown gravy, creamy mashed potatoes, several salads, and pumpkin pie that was stringy from freshly picked pumpkins. Grandma Thelma always made her special punch with lime sherbet. And there was her "famous" jam cake with brown-sugar icing and apple-stack cake towering many layers high.

I was fortunate enough to have two sets of grandparents, and the smell of yeast brings me right back to my grandma Young. She'd have biscuits baking in the oven, and I'd be on her lap looking at her birthstone pendant representing twelve children—one of whom was my mom. The icy lavender-blue color of February's amethyst birthstone represented my mom's birth and sparked childhood stories.

My mom carried on the tradition of holiday specialties with Christmas fudge from marshmallow crème or peanut-butter fudge and bourbon balls. Needless to say, the family always looked forward to these with great anticipation.

To this day, Christmas is not Christmas without Mom's candies. I can smell and taste each bite. In recent years she's taken to marinating maraschino cherries in Makers Mark Bourbon and then dipping them in melted chocolate, appropriately naming them "cherry bombs"!

Food for Homecomings

You've probably figured out by now that my family has to eat at every gathering, whether celebration or crisis. It's the first thing we think to do. When I get ready to go home, my sisters and mom talk recipes before the visit, ask me what I want to eat, and then schedule who's hosting me for dinner and on what night. It's just our excuse to get everyone together. And no matter what time I arrive from the airport, there's food waiting.

When Dad neared the end of his first prison term, he was elevated to the honor dorm where he could have contact visits. We were allowed to bring him food on Friday nights as long as it was in an official store box with a receipt. So we'd take him a BLT from the grocery deli and replace the tomato with one of our farm-fresh ones. Or we'd buy a pie from Kroger and replace a piece or two of it with Grandma Thelma's butterscotch pie or German chocolate cake. Those simple, thoughtful acts made his week.

My three children and I took a road trip to Kentucky on March 31, 2006, for Dad's release.

My three children and I took a road trip to Kentucky on March 31, 2006, for Dad's release. We packed the car with snacks: peanut butter and jelly sandwiches, Gatorade, Pepperidge Farm Pretzel Goldfish, apples, bananas, Fig Newtons, and Slim-Fast! Meal Bars for good measure. We drove nearly twenty-four hours straight through from Colorado to Kentucky. And as the miles flew by, we ate, played games, laughed, and bonded like you can only do when you're trapped together in a car. We arrived in Waynesburg at 3:00 AM, caught three hours of sleep, and then got up for the long-awaited drive to the prison. Mom, my sisters, nephew Jeremy, cousins, and our kids, all caravanned to the chain link fence and guard stations. Two white vans pulled up, about five men got out; one of them was Dad. We all welcomed him back. He didn't know I was coming; he cried.

Our first stop was Shoney's buffet in Danville, Kentucky. Dad wanted real bacon, real eggs, waffles, syrup and a cold glass of milk. (In prison they served only powdered milk at room temperature.) We piled up our plates and just watched him eat. We laughed, told stories, and reveled in having our Dad back home. Afterward, we went to the Walmart and bought him pants (*not* khaki), shoes, a shirt, and underwear; Jeremy got Dad fishing equipment so he'd be ready for his new life.

There's a Story Behind Every Meal

Some years ago a colleague and fellow foodie, Diane Passno and I, began to follow a column in our local newspaper, the *Tri-Lakes Tribune*, featuring food and the people and stories behind it. I had grown up with our local Kentucky paper the *Interior Journal*, which regularly profiled my Grandma Thelma's writing about potlucks and other food-centric events, and so this new column appealed to me.

Diane and I joked that we needed to kill off the columnist and take her job. (Given my family history, it's probably not wise to joke about these kinds of things.) We jabbed each other about it so much that when the columnist actually died, we met up and said, "Did you do it?" and "No . . . did you do it?" Soon afterward and still awash in guilt, we approached *The Tri-Lakes Tribune* and applied for the job. Much to our delight, the newspaper hired us—and Cooks on the Loose was born.

Diane and I profiled average, everyday folks for almost three years. We featured all sorts of people, such as the sweet woman who served us her mom's meatloaf on her mom's china. We wrote about her life and her childhood, and of course, we included her mom's recipe. We met people in their homes and in their restaurants. We featured the stories behind the meal, the cooking, the sights and smells—everything that tied the food to the people who created it.

We all have memories, and many of them are attached to food. We don't all have to be foodies to have the smells of Thanksgiving remind us of days when our grandparents were alive and family gathered around. I have learned how important it is to recount these stories and traditions to our children and our grandchildren, so they'll have a connection to the past.

OVERNIGHT MONKEY BREAD

No funeral is complete without food—especially overnight monkey bread.

Ingredients
- 1 package of frozen, round dinner rolls (I use Rhodes brand.)
- 3.5-ounce package butterscotch pudding (*not* instant)
- $1/2$ to 1 cup pecans (chopped or whole, your choice)
- $1/2$ cup margarine (*not* butter)
- $1/2$ cup brown sugar

Directions
1. Arrange 18 rolls in a buttered Bundt pan. Sprinkle with pudding plus pecans. Combine margarine plus sugar, boil until mixture becomes a caramel sauce (about 10 minutes) stirring often.
2. Pour sauce over rolls.
3. Cover with towel or plastic wrap and let stand overnight.
4. Bake at 350 degrees F for 25 minutes. Let stand for 10 minutes.
5. Run a knife around edge to loosen and invert onto serving dish.

nine

Matriarchs and Such

Endurance is not just the ability to bear a hard thing,
but to turn it into glory.

—PHILIP YANCEY, *Disappointment with God*

I was born on a gray, drizzly day that also happened to be the opening day of squirrel season. (Yep, they're eaten in Kentucky.) I know this because while Mom was in labor with me, Dad asked if it was okay if he left to go hunting with a friend. (Of course he did . . . but I digress!) It was Diana's first day of school, and Sherri was still a baby.

Mom had spent the previous day mopping, cleaning the house, and doing laundry. Back then, she filled the old Maytag Wringer Washer with water and washed the clothes. Then she took the rinse water, added a little bleach, and used the wash water to mop the floors. So resourceful!

I was born at 1:15 PM. Mom lamented that the only drug available in 1962 was ether—and that I came out of the womb with a mop of shocking black hair. I was such a long baby that Dad swiftly nicknamed me Tootie after the officer named Gunther Toody on the sitcom *Car 54, Where Are You?* In a journal entry from that era, Mom wrote that God knew me best as Toots.

Mom's Legacy of Commitment and Graciousness

Mom's name is Yvonne, but she's better known as Vonna Jean. She has always been a hard worker. In terms of her parenting, I caught far more than I was taught. Some of my sweetest memories are of being in the local Christmas plays with Mom. We shared mother-daughter roles and practiced our lines together. Mom played games and sang songs with me. And we'd stand on the hearth every Saturday, and each of us girls, Mom included, would take our turns at singing or dancing in tune with *American Bandstand*.

I've tried to hold my head up high during humiliating circumstances, as Mom has done.

I learned to find the humor in the midst of crisis and sorrow from observing my mom. I've tried to hold my head up high during humiliating circumstances, as Mom has done. I've persevered in hardship and valued the word *commitment*. I've learned to hold things loosely, to keep short accounts, and to seek God's heart. And just like Mom, I've overcome tough childhood circumstances that bred deep insecurities in me. Perhaps most important, though, I've learned about the power of prayer and loving others as God loves me. Pretty darn blessed, huh?

I've usually thought of my mom as an extraordinary woman in her Christian journey, but watching her handle certain events has taken my breath away and caused me to wonder, *Could I do that?* One of those happenings involved Dad's third wife, Red. Red came from a childhood of sexual abuse, prostitution, and general brokenness. She was a heavy drug user, and she and my dad partied together down by the river with others who lived in shacks. Red had six children by six different men; I remember meeting her nine-year-old boy who had a marijuana-leaf tattoo on his calf. It was a sad scene all the way around.

One evening, August 17, 1996, Dad came late to a party at a friend's house, and he found Red in bed with another man. Dad stormed out of the party and drove home to get a sawed-off shotgun. He returned to the scene wild with anger. The police report notes that he pulled up the driveway in his car and verbally threatened the man. Apparently the man yelled back and jumped on the hood of Dad's car. That's when Dad lifted his gun and blew a hole through the windshield and into the man's chest. The police found Dad hiding behind my grandparents' house.

This was Dad's first trip to prison. He got ten years for first-degree manslaughter because his blood alcohol level was higher than 2.0—that's above the average blackout level for those of you uninitiated with the heavy drinking scene. I think they were lenient on him. Red visited him in prison while he was awaiting trial. Even though he was angry enough to kill the man, somehow he forgave Red, and they never spoke of it.

Dad asked me to keep an eye on Red after he went to the penitentiary—and to reach out to her and her kids. I tried my best to fulfill his wishes. I sent them books, children's videos, and tapes from Focus on the Family, and I sent encouraging letters. It was tough from Colorado, though . . . so I enlisted Mom to reach out as well.

Asking Mom to help Red was asking a lot. The one time I hadn't seen Mom bounce through a hardship was in the wake of her divorce from Dad. She pined away for him, believing that God would honor her commitment and heal her marriage. In fact, the night Dad asked for a divorce, Mom spent nearly twenty-four hours afterward on her knees crying out to the Lord and searching the Scriptures for God's promises.

Her nervous breakdown followed. My request to reach out to Red came some twenty-plus years after the divorce, but it was still a huge request—one that would put into practice her ability to embrace grace and forgiveness. She takes everything to God through prayer, and when He has impressed on her heart to act, she acts!

After some spiritual wrestling, Mom decided to meet with Red at Oran's Truck Stop in Eubank, Kentucky. Their meeting was somewhat awkward, but Mom broke the ice by bringing Red a small gift, her own Bible, and by talking to her about the importance of marriage and parenting differently from how Red had been raised. Despite Mom's lingering desire for and grief over Dad, she told Red, "He needs you more than ever now. He needs to know he can trust you again."

Mom told me later that Red was "wild as a buck, the wildest thing I ever did see" and that Red didn't think church people would accept her. Mom shared a clear presentation of the gospel.

After of their meeting, Mom and I both received thank-you notes from Red. Here's the one she sent to Mom:

Yvonne,

Just a few lines to let you know how grateful I am for you and Tootie. There should be more people like you in the world; it would be a better place (in my eyes). There were many things I could have said to you at Oran's. I get a lump in my throat when it comes to Sharon Dale. I love and am in love with him. I believe you can relate with me that he sits on a pedestal. You must be a very strong woman, and I'm glad to have had the pleasure to meet you. Thank you very much for caring.

Sincerely,

Lenora Greer (Red)

Two weeks later Red was killed on the highway. We grieved this tragedy, but to this day Mom and I believe that God in His infinite mercy saved Red from herself and took her home.

Dad was devastated, of course. And Mom and we three daughters rushed to his side. Mom felt that God was calling her to continue to share the gospel with Dad. She drove three hours round-trip every Sunday. She purchased countless bags of Bugles corn snacks, Little Debbie Honey Buns, and Sprites from the vending machines during visitation. Mom remained a friend to Dad and thought he'd come back to her when he got out of jail.

After all these years—and another prison stint—she has finally accepted a life without him. I speak for all three of us daughters when I say, "Thank God!"

Mom's Joy

Mom is a funny ha-ha woman. We have laughed more than we've cried. When life is hard—which it often is—it helps to get through it with a good, hard cackle. And for a seventy-five-year-old, Mom is still a prankster. She's not as active as she used to be because of health problems and age, but she is still a faithful prayer warrior who shares the gospel and biblical wisdom with each and every family member. (She's been my own personal Bible Answer Man for years. Her depth of scriptural understanding blows my mind.) She also has an incredible relationship with my beloved nephews, Shane and Jeremy. Mom is their confidant and talks to them almost daily. In return they bring her the spoils of their hunting trips and often stock her fridge. She shares whatever she has with her neighbors. There are two women in her complex; one is a single mom with a severely disabled son. When Mom cooks, she usually makes enough to feed the other two women and their children. They reciprocate as well.

Mom has her flaws just like the rest of us. But I'm a far better person because of knowing her.

I don't mean to paint a picture of my mom as some saint with a glowing halo. She's not; none of us is. Mom has her flaws just like the rest of us. But I'm a far better person because of knowing her. I can't imagine life without Vonna Jean.

Mom's Childhood

Mom was the oldest of twelve children. Her job as the eldest was to take care of her younger siblings while Grandma Young cooked and took care of the house. Neither of her parents showed much affection, so that's something Mom had to do differently with her brothers and sisters and her own children.

Their family was dirt poor, and her Dad drank. He was meaner than the dickens. He'd come over the hill after an afternoon of drinking, and Grandma Young would ask my mom to get all the children to a safe place. Grandma wasn't safe from Papaw's abuse, and neither were their kids.

After Mom was married and pregnant with my oldest sister, Diana, she lived with her parents while my dad was away in the Air Force. One night Papaw Young came after her and knocked her down onto the couch. Mom immediately packed up and went to live with the Greer side of the family. She determined in her mind to make a peaceful, safe home for her family, and that did not include drunken violence.

In the summers Mom and her siblings played kick the can and the card game Rook. They would sneak off to the pond to swim. They were a musical family with each sibling more talented than the next. They harmonized to a level that rivaled the Partridge Family. (A few of the siblings now have a band called CrackerDarrel and the CrackerJacks—you can even like them on Facebook.) Mom remembers spending summer evenings on my grandparents' front porch, eating homemade ice cream while her brothers and sisters sang hymns, bluegrass, and country music together. Mom says they were also a family that could laugh a lot over nothing.

Grandma Young rarely had the ingredients to cook a proper meal. They ate what they grew and gathered from the land. Grandma got up at four or five in the morning, wrung the necks of chickens, and dipped them in boiling water a few times to get rid of the feathers, and then fried them up with homemade gravy and biscuits—all this work was accomplished before breakfast. The Youngs also ate many meals of pinto beans, potatoes, and corn bread until the gardens came in and provided an assortment of vegetables. Grandma Young had the incredible ability to take a single pot roast and feed not only her twelve children but also their spouses and kids. She fed the multitudes with one roast, a few potatoes, and a skillet of corn bread!

Mom's Faith

Mom was baptized when she was fourteen years old. She has often lamented that back then there were no classes on how to live a Christian life. She didn't understand that Jesus Christ—as they sang in the hymns—hung on an old, rugged cross to take the sins of the world on His shoulders and to create a bridge between human beings and God. She also was unaware that she could have a personal relationship with God and entrance into heaven by believing in His work on the cross.

Mom came to a saving knowledge of Christ one rainy evening. She, my dad, and some friends were drinking beer and driving along wet, dangerous back roads. She got scared and prayed, *God, if You get us home safe, I'll give up this kind of living. I'll live for You.* She got home safely that night and committed her life to God. Two weeks later Dad confessed to an affair. For over a year he wrestled with the idea of leaving us. Finally, he asked for a divorce.

It wasn't long before Mom felt strongly called to go talk with her father, Papaw Young, about her new faith. Papaw Young had gotten sober by that time. He was a different person, one who was funny, filled with song, and would give you the shirt off his back. This is how she described the encounter:

> I got up one morning, and the Lord wouldn't even let me drink my coffee. I knew I had to drive straightaway to his house. When I got

there I said, "Dad, I haven't even had my coffee this morning because the Lord impressed something upon my heart. Let me ask you a question: Am I going to see you in heaven?" And he said, "Why, Yvonne, I took care of that years ago."

After my twins were born, all the life lessons and values Mom instilled in me—and all that I caught without realizing it—began to manifest with my own children. There was a lot of dysfunction in my family, but it also had good in it. I am blessed to have come from such a rich background of faith, humor, and love—I now see Vonna Jean's legacy in action in the relationship between my own daughter Lee and her two boys.

"DON'T GET ATTACHED TO THE FAMILY PET" FRIED CHICKEN

To this day, I don't get attached to animals because they may end up on my dinner table. And yes, I have eaten squirrel.

Ingredients
- 3 eggs
- $^1/_3$ cup water
- 2 cups self-rising flour
- 1 teaspoon black pepper
- House Seasoning—recipe follows
- 1 (1 to $2^1/_2$-pound) chicken, cut into pieces
- oil, for frying, preferably peanut oil (which burns at 450 degrees F)
- optional: 1 cup, more or less, hot red pepper sauce
- special equipment: deep-fry thermometer

Ingredients for House Seasoning
- 1 cup salt
- $^1/_4$ cup black pepper
- $^1/_4$ cup garlic powder

Directions

1. Mix house seasoning in a bowl or plastic bag. Set aside.
2. In medium-size bowl, beat eggs with water. If desired, add enough hot sauce so egg mixture is bright orange.
3. In another bowl, combine flour and pepper.
4. Season chicken with House Seasoning by rolling in bowl or shaking in bag.
5. Dip seasoned chicken in egg mixture, and then coat well in flour mixture.
6. Heat oil to 350 degrees F in a deep pot. Do not fill pot more than $^1/_2$ full with oil. Make sure oil doesn't get too hot, because it will smoke black and let off a foul smell.
7. Fry chicken in oil until brown and crisp. Dark meat takes longer than white meat. It should take dark meat about 13 to 14 minutes and white meat around 8 to 10 minutes. Check with a meat thermometer to make sure it's done (180 degrees).

ten

Parenting: Only for the Brave of Heart

When my kids kissed me impetuously, I would never have said,
"Later. Now go get washed up for dinner."
—Erma Bombeck, "If I Had My Life to Live Over"

I love being a mom. I have even cherished the roller coaster of emotions that each new year, new day, and new hour bring. Let's face it: One minute you're in a misty-eyed haze of proud parenting, and in the next breath you're frazzled, calling out prayers, or staving off murderous thoughts. But in the end, somehow, someway, and by the sheer grace of God, everyone emerges alive and in one piece—at least that's how it's been for us.

I have a tight relationship with all three of my young adult children. My friends ask Tommy and me how we did it . . . how we successfully navigated the child-rearing years . . . how each of our children has a growing, vibrant faith . . . and even what the secret is to our teenagers' seeking to spend time with us and include us in activities with their friends. While it is remarkable, it certainly hasn't been an easy road. We are not perfect. Our children are not perfect. The five of us have made a heckuva lot of mistakes along the way.

In this chapter I'll talk a little about our parenting philosophy and what I believe made us successful. When my twin girls were babies and I was pregnant with my son, Buck, parenting seemed like a maze of dos and don'ts from well-meaning friends and family members. I felt overwhelmed by the multitude of parenting techniques, talking-head films, and philosophies that were available. Tommy and I knew we needed help, but we were careful not to get pigeonholed into "one right way."

I was fortunate, of course, to end up at Focus on the Family. I learned from the best minds in the family-helps field. Tommy and I, cognizant of our broken backgrounds, read everything we could get our hands on. We also prayed a lot, searched the Bible for answers, and acted and reacted from instinct. Most of all, we enjoyed our children and took an interest in their day-to-day activities. By prioritizing regular communication, we built strong, storm-resistant relationships.

Being There

I've been a working-outside-the-home kind of mom for the majority of my kids' lives. I truly believe having one parent stay home during children's formative years is the best-case scenario, but it's not an option for many families today. And it wasn't an option for us.

Yet Tommy and I made it work. He'd pick up the kids at school, and they'd go with him to his work sites. He was also master of the yearly ritual of back-to-school clothes shopping. He'd sit in a chair outside the dressing room and pass judgment on each outfit as it was displayed on the "models." And my role was to hold my kids when an offense from a friend brought waves of tears. We were a team—a team driven by intentionality, fun, and discipline.

Since Tommy and I both worked outside the home, we made a point to spend time with our kids, making the most of each evening and weekend. We invested in our kids' lives and fostered their interests. For example, Buck wanted to be a firefighter since he was a little boy. I knew how much it meant to him. So whenever I went on a business trip, I'd find the local fire station in whatever city I was in—often with a car filled with colleagues and the vehicle still rolling. We'd pull up, and I'd jump out and dash in for a special local patch.

Tommy and I have also been intentional about teaching our kids to be self-sufficient and wise.

Tommy and I have also been intentional about teaching our kids to be self-sufficient and wise. Throughout their lives we've played the Helen Keller game. Yes, Helen Keller, the deaf and blind heroine. Nearly every time we went to an airport or through the mall, I'd pretend I was blind and deaf like this great woman of faith. Okay, not very sensitive, but we didn't make a joke out of it. In this elaborate ruse, the kids would be charged with taking my hand and leading me to the gate, baggage claim, or the mecca of all shops, Mrs. Fields. This required solving problems, asking for directions, and stepping outside their comfort zones.

Years later as older teens, Buck and Lauren traveled internationally on mission trips and led their peers confidently through customs. They attributed their confidence to the Helen Keller competition. In fact, Lauren claims she'd *still* be in Peru if it weren't for the training our game gave her.

One Size Does Not Fit All

Regardless of whatever technique you adopt, remember, one size does not fit all. This has been the best parenting advice I've ever received. As the parents of twin girls and a son just a year younger, Tommy and I started out both praising and disciplining them together. It sure is easier to send everyone to his or her room rather than trying to sort out the morass of emotions and the "he said, she said" of four-year-olds. But the crucial lesson I learned early on was that they're all individuals. My twins are connected on a deeper level than Tommy and I can comprehend, but they are very different from each other. They have definite dislikes and likes, interests, weaknesses, and strengths.

As they grew up, I discovered the best environment for getting each one to open up and share his or her feelings. Buck shared the most with me in the kitchen, either unloading the dishwasher or helping me chop veggies. The longer he spent with me in the kitchen, the more he talked about his day and shared his thoughts.

Lauren, on the other hand, didn't want any part of the kitchen. Her place was lying on my bed just before Tommy and I went to sleep. She'd open up while she snuggled with us, talking, laughing, and sharing secrets. Lee was a tougher nut, not always wanting to chat, so often I'd have to get the lowdown from her sister, who always stood ready to spill the beans. (I should mention that Lee and I are alike!)

One regular practice I instituted early on was keeping a little notebook by each of our beds. The notebook was for everyone else to leave notes of encouragement, Scripture verses, pictures, or sometimes even apologies. Now that they're older, the kids treasure these tokens from their childhoods.

Life Lessons

We're churchgoers. Tommy and I recognized early in our lives of faith the importance of gathering once or twice a week with other believers. Even on Sundays when we would have rather stayed in bed, we roused the troops. For years our Sunday routine consisted of Tommy's cooking breakfast, eating together around the table, and then lying around the living room with different sections of the newspaper, chatting about the latest. Then we'd head to the eleven o'clock service.

When the girls were little, I lied and told them that when they lied, a little dot that only I could see would appear on their foreheads. I also told them that God and I talked. I don't know whether I'd recommend this advice, but it worked. The girls laugh about my methods now and will most likely pass on this bit of trickery. On the other hand, when my kids were teens (and even now), they couldn't keep things from me. "Mom always knows somehow," Lauren has always said.

When my kids were teens (and even now), they couldn't keep things from me. "Mom always knows somehow," Lauren has always said.

I raised my kids to know the value of confession and to keep short accounts with those who wronged them. I instituted a regular practice of asking them if their slate was clean. This is our family's way of asking if there is anything standing between them and their relationship with God and/or one another. This practice of asking—and listening to their responses—sparked lively discussions. Tommy and I were open as well; we encouraged the kids to ask about our slates, and we gave them answers appropriate for their ages.

This routine became more and more important as the kids aged. When they were young they played in a big creek behind our Colorado Springs home. Sometimes they'd come up to the house with snakes wrapped around their arms and necks and with assorted bugs in glass canning jars. But at about age nine or ten, they stumbled upon pornography. I remember the afternoon clearly. All three of them came barreling into the house, white-faced and out of breath. Lauren, our talker, explained what happened while the others looked at the ground, shifting back and forth on their feet. They had found a magazine in the bushes, and from their description it was clear they had come across hard-core porn. They didn't linger over it but tore up the magazine and buried it in different places so no one else would find it.

With sadness in my heart, I realized their innocence was gone. A year later Buck developed a problem. He and boys from school found porn online, and then Buck pulled it up on our computer. The salacious ads that popped up when we turned on the computer were our first indication that something was amiss.

It rocked our family. Tommy was livid. The night it happened he told the kids that instead of checking the windows and doors before bedtime, we were leaving them open so a prowler could just stroll in. We didn't actually do this. We simply wanted to give them a word picture so they could feel what it's like to open the door to evil.

Buck was remorseful, and we tightened the leash and held him accountable for his thought life after this incident. Two years afterward, though, Buck came downstairs in the early hours of the morning. Tommy and I were on the couch reading. As I looked up, I noticed something was wrong. He sat down next to me, put his head in his hands, and started crying.

He said, "I need to talk to you about my slate. I have a problem. I'm looking at pictures online. Tony (the director of our church's Easter play) asked us all if there was anything between us and God, and I knew I needed to confess to you and Dad." Since then Buck has been pure in body and spirit—as has his fiancée—and he knows he always has to be on guard against temptation and be held accountable. The hardest step for anyone in an area of addiction is confessing it. Getting the issue out in the open is critical.

Family Time

There's my work and Tommy's work, and then there's hunting season. This was a regular topic of conversation when I first met my husband. The fact that I had grown up as a hunter's daughter set me apart from the pack in Tommy's mind from the very beginning. The memory of my father and his faithful hunting buddies growing their ceremonial beards has stayed with me since my Kentucky childhood. According to Dad and his friends, beards provided warmth in the cold Kentucky mountains.

Every year as hunting season approached, the kids and I would prepare to be abandoned for a period of time. I used to call myself a hunting widow! Yet even hunting became a family affair. The conversations about planning meals, applying for tags, checking gear, and digging out the familiar always-in-fashion hunting togs kept the entire household in eager anticipation. I think the buildup to the hunt was as exciting as the hunt itself. And then as each of the kids aged, they tagged along with Tommy on their first hunting adventure. At the end of the trip, he would come home, wild game in hand, and it would populate our freezer and dinner plates in the months ahead.

We made a point of including our children in activities, and we enjoyed spending time with them and their friends.

Our family hunting memories are standouts, but there are many, many others. We made a point of including our children in activities, and we enjoyed spending time with them and their friends. We became the house on the block known for good snacks. We organized neighborhood block parties. We'd load a bunch of kids in the back of our pickup, bundle them in blankets, foist hot chocolate on them, and drive them around to see the lights at Christmas. Or we'd four-wheel-drive through an empty field doing donuts, giving our kids and their friends the ride of their lives.

We've started food traditions with our kids around Christmas. We make "Christmas mice" for all of our neighbors: Dip a stemmed cherry in melted milk chocolate, and while it's still warm, stick a Hershey's Kiss on the front. Then let it harden and use sliced almonds for the ears and red gel for the eyes and nose. We also dip Ritz Crackers in melted white chocolate during the holidays—much better than it sounds!

If you ask Lee, Lauren, and Buck, they'll tell you we were a house of fun. For years we had a bathroom in our "Chickweed House" that was unfinished and taken down to the drywall. One day I put magic markers on the counter and told the kids to decorate the walls. I also recorded their growth spurts on those walls. What's funny is that their friends—and our friends—started spending a lot of time in the bathroom. People would come over for dinner, excuse themselves, and come back fifteen minutes later after writing a limerick or their innermost thoughts on the walls.

Whether we were hunting, drawing on walls, or making holiday memories, the goals were always the same: We sought to make our children social, outgoing, and fun, all the while helping them become leaders with integrity.

Discipline

Tommy and I learned as parents that in this day and age you have to be ahead of the learning curves. You have to be the captain of the ship. If you're merely passengers, the boat will sink fast. What are the trends? What are your kids' friends talking about? Are you your kids' Facebook friend? Do you have your kids' password? Technology doesn't come naturally to some of us, but we have to adapt.

Tommy and I have tried not to swing too far one way or the other on the discipline pendulum. We've tried to parent with humility, remembering our own shortcomings and always wanting the best for our kids. We've grounded, spanked, and threatened. My children will tell you that I've yelled, but Tommy has been worse: He just shoots looks of disappointment. We've apologized to our children after losing our tempers. My children will also say that times of discipline have always been followed up with hugs, laughter, and getting life back to normal. We don't draw things out!

As you'll see in the coming chapter about my daughter Lee, even the best communication and a great relationship with your kids does not mean they won't falter or make grave mistakes. We do the best we can as parents to guide and instruct, and then we place them in God's hands. And as the Lord does with us, we walk with them through the rough patches.

CHRISTMAS MICE

Even though we move a lot, former neighbors track us down and ask for more Christmas mice.

Ingredients
- 1 package brown Hershey's Kisses (If you use the white ones, use white chocolate for the next ingredient. The white ones come out looking a bit like lab rats.)
- 12 ounces brown-chocolate melting dip
- 1 10-ounce jar (30 or so) maraschino cherries
- 1 cup sliced almonds, *not slivers*
- 1 small tube of red gel icing

Directions
1. Melt dipping sauce in microwave.
2. Dip cherry into melted chocolate (the mouse's body and tail) and attach a Hershey's Kiss (for the head) by pushing it gently into the coated cherry. Don't dip the Kiss into the chocolate, because it will melt, and you'll have an odd-shaped head.
3. Attach two sliced almonds for the ears.
4. Open red gel icing by piercing tip with a pin; you want a small hole for the opening. Use red gel icing to make dots for the eyes and nose.

Unshakable Grace

Forgiveness is the name of love practiced among people who love
poorly. The hard truth is that all of us love poorly . . . We need to
forgive and be forgiven every day, every hour—unceasingly. That
is the great work of love among the fellowship of the weak that is
the human family.

— HENRI J. M. NOUWEN, *The Only Necessary Thing:*
Living a Prayerful Life

*I*t will quickly become clear that I wanted to dazzle you with a chapter on our fine parenting skills before heading into murky waters. But here it is: a firsthand account of what many parents would consider one of their worst nightmares—and how grace transformed our family in the midst of it.

On a cold Colorado January night three days before my dad's infamous shooting, I waited for Lauren and Lee (now twenty years old), and my son, Buck, to join me for a Kentucky feast. Whenever health-conscious Tommy is out of town, the cast-iron skillets crawl out from the cabinets, and everything is fried, from bologna to chicken to potatoes.

Lee was the first to arrive home with her boyfriend, JP, sheepishly in tow. I could tell something was wrong when she walked through the door and darted into the bathroom. I asked JP what had happened. He didn't say anything, but I noticed his bottom lip quivering. Finally, Lee came out of the bathroom, crying. Honestly, I had zero clue. Did they wreck the car?

I turned off the stovetop and sat with Lee. She folded herself over and sobbed. I sat with my arms around her and laid my head on her back. "What on earth has happened?" I asked.

Through tears she raised up and said, "Mom, you're gonna kill me. You're just gonna kill me . . . I'm pregnant."

I paused for several seconds, took in a deep breath, and as if I were on autopilot, said, "Whatever happens from this moment forward, I love you, Lee."

At this point you might think that I shouldn't have been surprised by the revelation. After all, teen pregnancy is epidemic in today's culture, even among Christians. And certainly with my past, I knew how vulnerable young people can be to sexual temptation. But in my mind, our kids were pure. They were on the traveling abstinence team in school! They taught at our local pregnancy center!

Through tears she raised up and said, "Mom, you're gonna kill me. You're just gonna kill me . . . I'm pregnant."

We were intentional about fostering healthy, loving relationships and great communication with them. I made a point to be in their business. We talked openly about everything.

You might also wonder how my response was so measured and calm during the moment of truth. My family, after all, is known for shooting first and asking questions later. I suppose my brain had rehearsed for years the what-ifs and what-ands of my own past—and what I wished would have happened when I was Lee's age and experienced my own first unplanned pregnancy. Of course, it's only by God's grace that I didn't strangle JP, the boyfriend, who was at this point laid out crying on the floor in the other room.

Yet I was calm in the weirdest, most organized, and clear manner. I felt like an experienced crisis-management counselor. For example, this is what I would do if your arm were blown off: I would try not to draw attention to the pulsating blood hitting me in the face. And then I'd calmly wrap a tourniquet at the point of bleeding. No screaming. No freaking out. So when Lee dropped the bomb, maybe it was shock that made me appear like the supercool mom in a Lifetime movie of the week; I don't know.

I asked all of the usual questions and reassured Lee that from this point forward, we were going to work this out as a family. I remember saying, "Lee, there are a lot of things about my life that you don't know. And there will come a day when I can fill in the gaps for you. But for right now, know that I have seen this movie, and it has a beautiful ending. Only now, you're the star of the show, not me."

After my speech we found ourselves at a lull, and being a good Kentucky girl, my mind immediately went to the fried chicken on the stove. We were going to need to eat—a lot. Then we'd need to breathe and talk through next steps—primarily how in the world we were going to break the news to Tommy. He was on a pheasant hunt in Kansas, due home the next day with fowl blood on his clothes and shotgun in hand.

It's only fair to mention that Lee and JP were both virgins before they engaged in sexual intercourse. JP had never even passionately kissed anyone before Lee. But then they started experimenting sexually. Then it became fun, and they enjoyed the closeness they felt with each other. In their utter stupidity—because I can't say ignorance—they failed to use effective birth control. (Just for the record, I had gotten in Lee's face repeatedly in the months leading up to this point and asked whether she and JP were sexually active. She lied to me, all the while living with debilitating guilt. In fact, Lee was convinced that I knew she was lying. But I didn't.)

Lee's twin, Lauren, and her boyfriend at the time arrived. Lauren was furious upon learning about Lee's condition. *Okay, here we go*, I thought. *More emotions have just arrived on the scene.* Lauren hurled words at Lee and JP, calling them liars, and worse. I swiftly took Lauren into the other room and said, "But for the grace of God, this could be your story. So stop hurling stones and get yourself together. And come back when you can show the grace this situation demands."

Buck called and said he wouldn't make it for dinner that night after all, but that he'd be home the next day. *Buck will want to kill JP*, I thought, *but I'll worry about that later.* So I passed out some forks, and the five of us sat there eating right out of the pans. There was some silence, some disbelief, even some laughter as we discussed the viable next steps.

Crying Out to God—Why?

As the girls washed dishes, I went off by myself to the bathroom, got down on the floor, and cried out to God. I was angry and hurt—and shocked that He would have allowed this story to repeat. I had prayed for years that this generational sin would not repeat.

On the cold, smooth tile floor, I asked the Lord, "Didn't I do all the right things? Haven't I prayed and worshipped and covered my children at every turn? I cried out, "I've served faithfully at Focus on the Family for eighteen years. I'm the Vice President of Sanctity of Human Life at Focus on the Family—we spearhead abstinence education, for heaven's sake—why couldn't ours be the family that kept a pure reputation?"

I had a three-alarm meltdown with God. But in my head I knew this wasn't His fault. It came back to the simple yet sometimes difficult reality of our free will.

Lee asked to sleep with me that night. It seemed like in mere moments, she had transformed from a strong, independent young woman into a fragile little girl. Lauren wanted to sleep with us too; they wanted to "hunker up," as we call it. We giggled for a while, stressed for a while, played out how and who would tell Tommy, and talked about having a baby. We said things like, "Let's hope and pray the baby doesn't have JP's mouth combined with Lee's mouth—it will be like a billboard, a gigantic volcano opening!" After the girls had fallen asleep, I cried through the night.

I had a three-alarm meltdown with God. But in my head I knew this wasn't His fault.

The next day I called Buck and asked him to meet me at work, not at home. I knew this would hit him hard. Predictably, his emotions included denial, shock, anger, and a deep well of grief. I held him as he cried and told him to get every last emotion out because when we got home, I needed him to be there for Lee. I also gave him the same speech as Lauren, "Only by the grace of God, this is not your story, Buck. I need you to walk into the house with grace in your heart." The emotional wreck who had cried herself to sleep the night before was gone, and the cool, calm, collected Lifetime Movie Network mom was back.

Finally, there was Tommy—the conversation we were all dreading. He was driving back from Kansas, and I went back and forth whether to share the news with him over the phone. On one hand, the phone seemed a little inappropriate for a life-altering chat—a cop-out, like breaking up with someone by text message. But I knew how Tommy processes information. And I wanted his first reaction—both verbal and the look on his face—to take place far away from our fragile daughter. I did not want Lee to live with the lifelong memory of her father's initial emotions—which I suspected were not going to be good.

Additionally, miracle of miracles, Tommy happened to be driving back with a marriage-and-family therapist, a good friend, from a large church in town. What a perfect setting in which to initially process this information, I thought. (Better that Tommy unload on the therapist than on me and Lee!)

So I called Tommy on my way home from work. He began talking on and on about the pheasant hunt. And as much as I tried to take an interest in my husband's impassioned account of birds, all I heard was static, lots of static. In fact, the only thing I could concentrate on was my stomach crawling up through my esophagus and knocking on the door of my throat. I felt gravely ill. At some point I interrupted and said, "There's something I have to tell you; it's about Lee."

Silence. Interminable silence. Tommy thought of one of the worst things that could happen and said slowly, "Did she have an abortion?" I said, "No, but she is pregnant." Again, silence. So I plowed ahead and recapped the previous night for him.

When I got home, I told Lee that I'd had the conversation with her father. A fresh wave of tears appeared, and all of us nervously awaited his arrival. Finally, we heard Tommy's truck pull in. We stood in silence, a tense line of nerves and grief. Tommy walked through the back door, and Lee ran immediately into his arms and started crying. He held her in silence.

> **Tommy walked through the back door, and Lee ran immediately into his arms and started crying.**

The next day, January 9, Tommy was not doing so well, however. The shock had worn off, and there was quite a bit of tension and silence. And Lee had officially regressed to the ripe old age of seven again, clinging to me like a child. As a family, we worked through nine months of these kinds of ups and downs.

The Other Big Reveal

Tommy and I had talked throughout the years about the appropriate time to tell the kids about my abortion and unplanned pregnancies. I wanted a clean slate with them. But I knew—and I was glad—that we decided Tommy should hold the keys to this news.

Early on I asked a wise friend about how, when, and what I should reveal. He told me to wait until our kids had a solid, mature relationship with God, because it could rock them to the core. And they needed a steady Rock to hold on to!

He also said to make sure that Tommy and I both had good communication and a strong, open relationship with our kids. He advised us not to reveal anything during a heated season of their lives. And he said, "Avoid discussion during hormonal adolescence, because in their understanding of their own sexuality, they may think, *Well, you did it, and it turned out okay.*"

On a Friday night midway through Lee's pregnancy, Tommy and I called a family meeting. We knew it was time. Buck and Lauren had lingering feelings of resentment that flared up from time to time. They felt betrayed by the lies. And Lauren, unbeknownst to us, was torn up inside that her twin and best friend was going to replace her with this new baby. We needed to clear the air.

Our time together started with Lee crying—a regular occurrence amid the morning sickness, the weighty decisions, the multitude of doctors appointments, the future. Tommy and I came alongside our girl, and we never let her falter. But we also let her feel the consequences of her actions. We didn't sugarcoat anything.

Through her tears Lee said that no one understood what she was going through, and that she felt utterly alone. That's when I spoke up. I started at the beginning. I talked about my promiscuous behavior prior to marriage, my abortion, and then the unplanned pregnancy with the twins. (I should mention that my girls take after me—we're dumb as rocks when it comes to math. Harsh, but true. Later Lee and Lauren said they had made calculations for years but couldn't quite get their conception, birthday, and my and Tommy's wedding date to jibe!)

The biggest decision Lee and JP made—and the one where Tommy and I held our tongues—was whether they should choose an adoptive family. And whether they should marry. I know that a number of teens richly bless barren couples with the gift of life. This is both admirable and amazing. It's just that I couldn't fathom my first grandchild in the hands of another grandma! Selfish, perhaps, so I didn't offer my thoughts on this subject. I will say that Tommy and I were delighted when they decided to keep the baby—and marry.

And then, like me, Lee walked down the aisle with a prominent baby bump at seven-and-a-half-months pregnant. The wedding was beautiful. The pastor who had married Tommy and me also married Lee and JP. Lee just wanted family and a few close friends at the service. One-hundred and fifty strong from both Tommy's and my clans came for ceremony. We also included Lona and her children since they were, of course, family.

I asked Lee, "Why are you crying on your wedding day?" And she said she didn't want to leave home—and her childhood—behind.

Lee and JP honeymooned in Mexico, but not before Lee came over to our house crying. I asked Lee, "Why are you crying on your wedding day?" And she said she didn't want to leave home—and her childhood—behind.

New Life

I wish Lee's birthing experience had been easy. One morning near her due date, Lee was over at the house and came downstairs to tell me that she had a *feeling* it was time. We called the hospital, and they told us to come in. I first painted her toenails—because you must have pretty toenails for a baby delivery.

We spent the next eighteen hours in a small room at Memorial Hospital. We played cards, worked on puzzles, and tried to read magazines to pass the hours. There was a lot of furious texting and Facebooking going on. Sometimes Lauren would wave a Snickers bar under Lee's nose, since she wasn't allowed to eat. A mass of people came and went from the birthing room to the waiting room. It was a well-attended event! And we were losing our minds with anticipation, excitement, and nervousness.

At some point the doctor came in and said that he didn't have hope that Lee would progress above four centimeters, and they needed to do an emergency C-section. Lauren cried. Lee had a panic attack, and they had to tie down her hands. I cried in JP's arms at the sight of my own baby in such distress. Tommy paced.

It was time. JP and I suited up in our green sterile attire.

They wheeled Lee into the operating room. JP held her hand, and I stroked her hair. They pulled out Landon Matthew Tomberlin for all of us to see at 6:20 AM on August 24, 2008. He was screaming like a banshee and seemed healthy in every way.

However, our rejoicing was short-lived. At the end of his initial testing, the doctors discovered that he had an E. coli bacterial infection. The nurse whisked him away saying six words a parent (or grandparent) *never* wants to hear, "We will do everything we can." They were worried that the infection would travel to his brain and progress to meningitis.

Landon remained in the neonatal intensive care unit (NICU) for twenty-three days. Leaving the hospital without her baby, remaining on bed rest in the wake of surgery, having us deliver her milk to the hospital, and seeing her baby with needles in his head (which delivered the antibiotic) changed Lee. I could see her dependence on the Lord increasing day by day. The faith of her childhood was becoming tangible.

Much to our relief—an understatement—Landon finally came home.

Rough Waters

JP and Lee went through some rough waters their first years of marriage with stresses involving money, work, and a new baby. But with the help of their family and our fabulous New Life Church (and a Beth Moore study or two for Lee!), they dug in their heels and made a commitment to see it through. And they're doing great. JP has stepped into his role as "a man after God's own heart," and we are so proud (1 Samuel 13:14).

I'm in awe of Lee and the amazing momma she's become. She loves her boys beautifully. And I'm not just speaking of JP and Landon. Early in 2011, they welcomed their second son, Jaxon Paul, into the world.

God allows trials of all sorts to come into our homes to strengthen us and our kids.

Beauty for ashes, indeed. I honestly don't know what our family would do without these bundles of complete and utter joy. Each of our worlds revolves around them—and they have brought us closer together as a family.

Is it irony or providence that Lee and I trod similar paths to motherhood? I can't answer that question. I do know that I was able to extend grace, mercy, and forgiveness because I had walked a mile in her shoes. I can also say with certainty that God can redeem any situation, no matter how bleak.

No matter how many things we do right as parents, stuff happens. God allows trials of all sorts to come into our homes to strengthen us and our kids. The best we can do is pray for the grace to handle these situations as they come our way and ask for the Lord's mercy and peace to be with us in the midst of the storms.

For Lee's version of the story, go to http://www.youtube.com/watch?v=E-gA5F2Nitk&feature=relmfu or go to You Tube and search for the terms "Focus on the Family unplanned pregnancy 2010."

CRISIS MACARONI AND CHEESE

Eat this straight out of the pan for comfort in any crisis.

Ingredients
- 1 pound elbow macaroni
- $^1/_2$ pound American cheese slices (or more if you like it über-cheesy)
- $^1/_2$ cup whole milk
- 3 tablespoons butter
- salt and pepper

Directions

1. Boil macaroni until done; pour off water, rinse, and drain.
2. Put back into pan and add $1/3$ of the cheese and milk. Stir until melted.
3. Add butter and remaining cheese and milk until all is melted.
4. Season with salt and pepper.

twelve

Still New Every Morning

You called; you cried; and you broke through my deafness.
You flashed, you shone, and you chased away my blindness.
You became fragrant; and I inhaled and sighed for you.
I tasted and now hunger for you.
You touched me and I burned for your peace.

—SAINT AUGUSTINE, *Confessions*

*M*y dad's imprisonment and other family tragedies, my daughter's pregnancy, and my marriage have all driven me to my knees in prayer. How could they not? I have known in each case that it is only by God's power—tapped through prayer and experienced in daily, minute-by minute dependency on Him—that I can make it through to the other side and even thrive in the midst of heartache.

There have been other crises—the daily stuff, from broken-down cars to Buck's relentless migraines and my mom's cancer to everything in between. For me even the little things hold the power to devastate my day, bring about depression, and cause me to completely lose perspective. The big things force me to my knees, but the little things offer me the choices to turn to Him or distract myself with busyness, food, shopping, television . . . you name it!

But most days now I live and breathe prayer—I have for years.

I can thankfully say I have an amazing life, and my husband, children, family, and friends are wonderful—but that's not enough. My relationship with Jesus is satisfying in ways that earthly relationships are not. And it was built, slowly but surely, by sharing everything with God through regular prayer.

As my life illustrates, there are not always storybook endings. My heart has broken over issues within my family.

Early in my faith, a nun at a local retreat center, Sister Mary Agnes, offered me a structure for my time with God. She suggested I open my prayers with praise to God, then present my petitions, followed by an Old Testament scripture such as a psalm, then a New Testament verse, then relinquishment or confession of sins, and finally sitting still before God. I have altered this pattern over the years. I'm not so rigid in my time with God. At the same time, I love the diversity of how and what I can do in prayer and the thought of how it honors God. I pray throughout the day, sometimes as a ceaseless conversation with God. Still, my prayers, like every parent's, must sound desperate and panicky to the Lord at times. I recall as if it were yesterday saying, "No, You can't take this baby." I knew in my head that He held the decision in His hands, but I refused to relinquish my first grandson. *Not my will, Lord, but Yours be done,* I prayed. It wasn't easy.

A Vibrant Relationship with Jesus

As my life illustrates, there are not always storybook endings. My heart has broken over issues within my family and with others whose lives seem hopeless in the face of struggles, such as addictions, unplanned pregnancies, and no money for baby food, to name a few. Some moms don't leave the hospitals with their babies. Some daughters don't have dads to love and hold them during the storms of life. I have had to learn and rely on the fact that I do have a faithful Prince of Peace who always rides in to save the day, to bring me joy, and to comfort my heart during unsettling times. This Prince was there all along, but it has only been through relationship that I've learned to recognize His presence and trust that He is good and wants the best for me. This friendship with God took time to build, and it takes time to maintain. But the following steps and practices continue to pave the way to a vibrant relationship with God.

Intentionality

Reaching a level of intimacy with God requires that I take intentional action. Similar to any other relationship, this one takes care, respect, and regular tending to. I share both my joys and sorrows—and even laugh with the Lord—knowing that He gets the joke and finds irony in much of what goes on in my life.

I have a terrible memory. I always tell people I forget things so easily that I can hide my own Easter eggs. I'm one of those people who needs to jot down notes in order to remember. From the very beginning of my journey with God, I have kept a prayer journal. I've seen that my words tell stories of God's faithfulness in the little and big events of my life. I write down prayers, hopes, and visions for the future. I note important scriptures that I meditated on day and night to get through a certain crisis. My faith is strengthened by going back through my journals and seeing how the Lord has answered prayer.

I've also made it a practice to carry around prayer index cards, each devoted to a different group of people in my life. I have ones for the Maher side of the family, the Greer clan, my close friends, my small group, my work colleagues, my marriage, my kids, and all of the folks in my life who have yet to trust Christ and His work on the cross.

I try to intentionally ferret out prayer needs in meetings with colleagues, on the phone with friends or family members, or even in new introductions. I especially like to do this with my kids before they embark on a new adventure. Days before Buck entered Air Force boot camp, I knew I had to pray that his migraines wouldn't interfere with his training. I also had him write down his every fear, every need, and every thought for me. His index card included such phrases as "sleeplessness," "to be able to perform more," "break habits that will impede success," "be a light for Christ to the other guys," "be a good leader." Boot camp has long since passed, but I have highlighted answered prayers in my journal that remind me that Buck started a Bible study among his peers, the headaches stayed at bay during his training, and he developed new, healthy habits during the eight-week period. In many ways, my Buck emerged from boot camp as a man. But I had to intentionally relinquish him and all his ways to the Lord. Prayer works, people!

Forgiveness

D. L. Moody said, "I firmly believe a great many prayers are not answered because we are not willing to forgive someone." This is a strong statement, eh? And it's especially poignant for those of us who have been deeply hurt. I wrote a little earlier about the process of forgiving my dad. Over time I've learned that unforgiveness impedes a relationship with God; I see it as prayer with a limp. So I do my best to keep short accounts. I don't do grudges well anyway—they fester and pollute everything in my path. I have had some amazing opportunities to practice this don't-hold-a-grudge thing! Even when I don't feel like it, I must forgive.

I have made my time with the Lord a nonnegotiable. Every morning before the busyness of the day begins, I start out asking God to search my heart, and I mean it. It's not a frantic, guilt-ridden search. However, I want to know if there is something that keeps me separated from Him, and I trust Him to reveal it. This is not because I'm superspiritual; it's because I'm super-freaked-out about the gazillion ways I've blown it! I need the clean slate.

I have made my time with the Lord a nonnegotiable.

A very hard discipline for me has been to forgive someone for an offense just after it happens, but I've learned this is critical. I think back to a time when a colleague shared something completely confidential about me in a group setting for the "benefit of others to pray for me." I initially ruminated on murderous thoughts and plotted a backyard burial for this colleague. My second reaction was hurt and deep humiliation. I had shared something personal, and now it was public. After time, discussion with trusted friends, and prayer, I knew I had to forgive and pray for this person. A wise friend said, "Heap blessings upon that person." This is a minor example; other more serious situations may include dealing with serious betrayal, rejection, and even physical and/or emotional abuse. But as difficult as this task may be, continuing to pray for your enemies and truly embracing forgiveness removes much of the sting. I promise! On my end, I sometimes need to ask the Lord for forgiveness for my own offenses every hour. Forgiveness isn't always easy—in fact, it's rarely easy—but it's necessary to keep life-giving, life-altering communication flowing with Jesus. I hit the spiritual ceiling in the midst of unforgiveness, and yet Jesus never shuts off His side of the conversation. He is always with me. It's the communication that keeps my heart flowing toward Him.

Obedience
Intimacy with Jesus requires that I do what He asks of me whether I feel like it or not. I've learned that obedience precedes emotion. If my feelings drive me, I'll never pray for certain people, especially those who have

wronged me in some way. There are days I don't feel like reading Scripture, journaling, fasting, or even expending the emotional energy to cry out to the Lord over something. Yet I know that obedience is required for intimacy with Christ—and that God honors my faithfulness both with His presence and with answered prayer. In fact, the days I least feel like seeking Him through prayer but do it anyway are the days I most often experience spiritual breakthroughs.

I've learned (yet again the hard way) that I have an obligation to act upon what the Lord shows me in prayer. This isn't always an easy path to walk, but it becomes easier as my relationship with the Lord grows and I realize I can trust Him with anything.

Relinquishment

It's amazing how readily I try to keep control of areas of my life without God's guidance. Even noble pursuits, such as weight loss, my children's and Tommy's welfare, and ministry to others, can become sinful if I don't allow the Lord to guide me. Those things can quickly become idols stealing my allegiance if I don't choose to place the Lord first.

Let's talk about weight loss, for example. I really need to be exercising and engaging in healthy habits. I say over and over to God, "Your will, not my will" on this issue. But I hate exercising, and I love eating and lounging around. Sometimes I embrace the motto, "I'll eat what I want, die young, and call it all good." I say this knowing food-related illnesses run in my family. Gout is especially popular among the Greers and Mahers. I imagine I'll have ten gout toes by the time I'm fifty-five because I refuse to relinquish shellfish and red meat, two culprits in the gout world. Mom has gout toes. Tommy has gout toes. My sister Diana and I battle it out over who's going to catch what first. The Lord knows this about me. He knows my weaknesses, and yet still He calls me His beloved child.

Again, if I ask the Lord to search my heart, He will be faithful to show me areas of sin and weakness. Then I can lay them down, knowing that I need His help to do this—and that I may need to give them to Him over again and again.

Embracing Brokenness in the Presence of Jesus

Since I've experienced my fair share of heartache in life, I don't like to willingly place myself in a position where I'm actively seeking out suffering and embracing it. Who would? In fact, I'd rather do about anything then face the tough stuff on a regular basis. I'm tired of the brokenness! Yet true humility before—and dependence on—God only comes by embracing brokenness and allowing Him to walk through it with me.

That process takes talking to the Lord in prayer about the ways I've been hurt—and the ways I've hurt others. It's confessing to Him my raw feelings, which may be disappointment in how He answered a prayer or the desert He seems to have me in. It's going to those dark places and allowing God to reveal His perspective on the situation. Sometimes the tough stuff comes up naturally after a hard week. Other times it happens by being intentional and asking the Lord to examine my heart and point me to a certain scripture. Truthfully, very few of us have to make much effort to bring brokenness to the surface.

I have also learned over time that when I've embraced brokenness, I've grown the most in my relationship with Jesus. I've gained trust in Him, and slowly I've learned how to open my heart to His healing, comfort, and peace. Embracing the path of brokenness offers benefits and gifts that money, "therapy shopping," and all of the counseling in the world can't buy.

Ministry

One of the other ways I have grown in faith is actively engaging in ministry to others as an outgrowth of my relationship with Jesus. I spent twenty years at Focus on the Family, mostly in outreach to other women. Through this work I was able to pour into others the love, compassion, hope, and wisdom that Jesus pours into me. What an incredible privilege!

Whenever I stand up in front of a group of women, sharing my testimony and mentioning my heartaches, my vulnerability opens the door for others to come forward and share their burdens with me, often as a first step toward emotional healing. And because I'm open to others, the Lord continues to bring strangers into my path, whether I'm on a plane, at the mall, or in line at the grocery store.

Ministry has permanently altered my perception of the value of my life and others. And it is another way God has revealed my weakness and healed me. One of my favorite Bible passages is Isaiah 58:6–8:

Is not this the kind of fasting I have chosen:
to loose the chains of injustice
    and untie the cords of the yoke,
to set the oppressed free
    and break every yoke?
Is it not to share your food with the hungry
    and to provide the poor wanderer with shelter—
when you see the naked, to clothe [them],
    and not to turn away from your own flesh and blood?
Then your light will break forth like the dawn,
    and your healing will quickly appear;
then your righteousness will go before you,
    and the glory of the LORD will be your rear guard.

In interacting with people of all stripes—including those I just want to strangle!—the Lord has brought issues to light that He wants to change within me. And through ministry He has also healed me of certain hurts in my past.

I hope that as you've read this book, you haven't seen me as someone who has it all figured out. My prayer is that you will see all this as a path to God's ongoing mercy and His grace.

New Every Morning

You know that awkward moment when you're writing a book that is being published by your employer, and your position is eliminated? You don't? Well I do! Yep, my twenty-year tenure at Focus on the Family ended as I clicked away at my keyboard. Talk about a shake up! Every thing was moving along beautifully in a job I loved, with people I had come to know as family. I was feeling as though I was walking on the very path God had put before me—then *kaboom!* I was flattened on every level. In the moments following my own personal "reduction in force," I was breathless, immobile—everything moved in slow-mo. Part of my identity was wrapped up in my career, and my children had grown up under the umbrella of my work at Focus; my job was part of their identity too! Even though my world was rocked to its core, I wasn't blindsided. I had experience under my belt with trusting God; I had thick skin, but I wasn't calloused. I did wrestle with being able to say, "not my will, Lord, but Your will be done." At the same time, I spoke out scriptures and exercised trust in the Lord for the future, even when I didn't feel it in my heart. I'll say it again: I knew my obedience needed to proceed my feelings. And I also knew that my God would not let my family and me fall.

During my twenty years at Focus on the Family, I learned so many of the lessons I've shared about how the Lord can and will use all types of people (donkeys included) to proclaim His truth. I not only talked about faith, but I also tried walking in faithful ways that lined up with my rhetoric. As I wrote about mercy and grace and learned that my employment was ending, I was forced to check my heart to see if I was willing to give that mercy and grace as well as wanting to receive it.

I've moved from what I call my "Focus stepping-stone years" (my first twenty years in a career) into another role that allows me to embrace my testimony and utilize my experiences from the school of hard knocks. Now as an associate pastor at my home church in Colorado Springs, I am able to speak about my life and God's mercies, as well as shepherd God's people on their journeys. And yes, I can now legally marry and bury. Call me if you need either service!

My broken past still has a tendency to stalk me as an adult, but the Lord continues to remind me that His grace is more relentless. I am thankful He made me His daughter and brought people into my path to show me how to seek Him. I am humbled that He has used my past hurts to also bring new healing in the lives of others. And I love that the Lord has replaced all of these ashes for beauty and for His glory!

GRANDMA THELMA'S HOT PANCAKE SYRUP

This syrup is a must-have on hotcakes slathered in peanut butter. Pray that it doesn't burn while you're making it.

Ingredients
- $1/2$ cup brown sugar
- $1/2$ cup granulated sugar
- $1/2$ cup water
- $1/4$ teaspoon vanilla
- 1 pinch salt

Directions
1. Combine all ingredients in a small microwave-safe measuring pitcher.
2. Mix until well combined.
3. Microwave for 50 seconds. Stir.
4. Microwave for 20–50 seconds more, or until mixture boils. Stir.
5. Serve hot or let cool.

Acknowledgments

*T*his has to be the most difficult part of writing this book! I've played it out in my mind in so many ways. *Should I make the acknowledgment page short and vague with mysterious gratitude to the "you know who you are" groups? Or should I make a long list of names but put them in a very cool and unique font?* Seriously, how does one thank the people who have sacrificed their time, their stories, and their gifts to allow someone else's life to become a book?

I have a lifetime of gratitude to and love for my family. To Mom, Dad, Diana, and Sherri: I wouldn't have chosen some of the journeys we've been on, but I wouldn't change them either. You are my strength. And I love you all beyond measure! We have learned how to survive with an abundance of grace, mercy, forgiveness, and great food. To the Greers and the Youngs: It is because of you that I have a love for music and laughter and the gift of bossing others around. You shaped me. Good, bad, or ugly—I am yours.

I owe an enormous thanks to my incredible husband Tommy! I wouldn't want to go through this life with anyone else! I'm honored to be your wife!

To our amazing kids Lee, Lauren, and Buck: You have allowed me to share some of our greatest joys and deepest hurts. My story is in part your story, and I love you all more than words can ever express. You are my badge of courage, my only claim to success.

To JP, Alecia, and to Lauren's future stud, welcome to our wonderfully crazy family!

I would never have had the courage to share this story if not for an amazing group of friends, past and present, who have gotten me through this life—literally. Gina, my sweetheart friend: I wouldn't have graduated high school if you hadn't let me cheat off you. Lona: Not only did you and your family take me in, feed me, and cover me in prayer; you are also my memory keeper. This book couldn't have happened without your sorting of the stories and the hurts that I had chosen to forget. I needed to remember them in order to fully embrace God's mercy. So thank you.

To the Maher family: You gave me Tommy and welcomed me with a loud, wonderful Italian heritage to pass on. You are my family that only the Lord knew I would be blessed with! I love you all!

To my Colorado friends: You are such a blessing to me and our family because you have been such a part of our story and our healing. You inspire me to live out my past through a filter of love and grace, with a heart for the future. You have loved us with too many wonderful memories to count. Thank you all for laughing, praying, and eating with me. Thanks also for indulging me with your love and encouragement.

To Focus on the Family: Thank you for what is equivalent to a PhD in learning the ways of leadership, management, HR, development, re-engineering, communications, and so much more! Twenty years of schooling have given me more blessings than I can count and more wrinkles than I care to acknowledge. I wouldn't trade a day for the friendships that you have given me.

To my Tyndale friends—Linda, Jeff, Mark, Jenni, Jackie, and all the rest of the bunch: I *love* the cover of this book! The only thing missing is my guitar and a hit song! Who knows? Maybe that's coming! You all are awesome, and if you market this book well, I'll love you even more. ☺

I'm saving this last bit of gratitude for my co-laborers on this book.

Amy Tracy: You rock my face off! You've listened to me, interviewed family and friends, traveled to Kentucky, and creatively pulled together a story of pain, love, forgiveness, mercy, and hope. Then you made it into a memoir. I will be forever grateful for your long hours and late nights of wrestling with these chapters. May this be the first of many "babies" you birth in your future of writing!

To the Focus book editors, freelancers, and marketing team who helped with this project: Marianne, Brock, Allison, Bruce, Chris, Larry, Robert, Angie, Norm, and Jeremy. Thank you for your enthusiasm and crazy-fun ideas for this book! Do I detect a little pent-up silliness? You are all out-standing in your creativity and editing skills! I'm so thankful that you all paid attention in school.

To anyone I've not mentioned by name: It may have been to protect your anonymity or your reputation. For others, it may be that I'm forget-ful; remember, I can hide my own Easter eggs. I love you nonetheless!

Thank you Burger House Restaurant in Lancaster, Kentucky, for the consistency in your hoagie basket. Will you ever give me the recipe?

For the men and women in our military: Thank you for your daily sacrifice. Thank you for our safety and for your families, who give up so much.

And last and certainly not least, for Your glory, Lord. Without You, none of this would have been possible.

Notes

Chapter 1

1. Philip Yancey, *What's So Amazing About Grace?* (Grand Rapids: Zondervan, 1997), 70.

2. Philip Yancey, *Finding God in Unexpected Places* (New York: Doubleday, 2005), 66.

Chapter 2

1. Eugene O'Neill, *The Great God Brown*, act 4, scene 1, http://gutenberg .net.au/ebooks04/0400091h.html.

Chapter 4

1. Donald Miller, *Through Painted Deserts*, (Nashville: Thomas Nelson, 2005), x.

Chapter 5

1. Frederick Buechner, *Telling the Truth: The Gospel as Tragedy, Comedy, and Fairy Tale* (New York: HarperCollins, 1977) 50.

2. Buechner, *Telling the Truth*, 56.

Chapter 8

1. Sara Covin Juengst, *Breaking Bread: The Spiritual Significance of Food* (Louisville: Westminster John Knox Press, 1992), 15.

2. Joyce Carol Oates, *A Widow's Story: A Memoir* (New York: HarperCollins, 2011), 149.

About the Author

Yvette Maher currently serves as associate pastor for the 50⁺ L.I.F.E. Ministry at New Life Church in Colorado Springs, Colorado. She previously served at Focus on the Family as the Senior Vice-president of Family Ministries as well as Senior Communications Specialist. In her twenty-year tenure, Yvette appeared frequently on the *Focus on the Family*® daily broadcast and *Weekend*® *Magazine*, authored many articles for Focus on the Family magazines, and served as host for the weekly webcast *Your Family Live!*™

She frequently speaks at women's conferences and retreats around the globe. Her engaging and humorous personality, along with knowledge of spiritual principles and truths, allows Yvette to encourage people to value their God-given design and to impact their homes, communities, and the world for Christ.

To contact Yvette for an event or share *your* stories of God's mercy, please email her at myhairgodsmercy@gmail.com. You can also follow Yvette on Twitter: @yvettemaher

FOCUS ON THE FAMILY®

Welcome to the Family

Whether you purchased this book, borrowed it, or received it as a gift, thanks for reading it! This is just one of many insightful, biblically based resources that Focus on the Family produces for people in all stages of life.

Focus is a global Christian ministry dedicated to helping families thrive as they celebrate and cultivate God's design for marriage and experience the adventure of parenthood. Our outreach exists to support individuals and families in the joys and challenges they face, and to equip and empower them to be the best they can be.

Through our many media outlets, we offer help and hope, promote moral values and share the life-changing message of Jesus Christ with people around the world.

Focus on the Family MAGAZINES

These faith-building, character-developing publications address the interests, issues, concerns, and challenges faced by every member of your family from preschool through the senior years.

For More INFORMATION

 ONLINE:
Log on to
FocusOnTheFamily.com
In Canada, log on to
FocusOnTheFamily.ca

 PHONE:
Call toll-free:
**800-A-FAMILY
(232-6459)**
In Canada, call toll-free:
800-661-9800

THRIVING FAMILY®	**FOCUS ON THE FAMILY CLUBHOUSE JR.®**	**FOCUS ON THE FAMILY CLUBHOUSE®**	**FOCUS ON THE FAMILY CITIZEN®**
Marriage & Parenting	Ages 4 to 8	Ages 8 to 12	U.S. news issues

Rev. 3/11